GW00500293

Reggie

Marix coat of arms as registered in the College of Arms, London.

Reggie

The Life of Air Vice Marshal
R L G Marix CB DSO

by

John Lea

The Pentland Press Limited
Edinburgh · Cambridge · Durham

Dedicated to Squadron Leader
Nigel Trevor Marix, RAF,
by his wife, The Honourable
Yvelyne de Marcellus Marix

First published in 1994 by
The Pentland Press Ltd.
1 Hutton Close
South Church
Bishop Auckland
Durham

ISBN 1 85821 170 1

Typeset by Elite Typesetting Techniques, Southampton.
Printed and bound in Great Britain by Bookcraft (Bath) Ltd

Contents

Introduction

Air Vice Marshal Reginald Lennox George Marix, CB, DSO, RAF – 'Reggie' to his friends, his Air Force colleagues, and his family – was born 17 August 1889, and died 7 January 1966. His service career began when he joined the Royal Naval Volunteer Reserve in 1909, and continued until his retirement in 1945. He was one of that small handful of pilots who learned to fly before World War One and remained on active service through World War Two.

Reggie Marix's service life spanned an era of spectacular development in aviation. His Reserve service began in the year Bleriot made history by flying the Channel. Just three years later, as a Sub Lieutenant RNR, he learned to fly on a Bristol biplane with a maximum speed of well below 100 mph. When he finally retired after all those years of distinguished and unique service, the Meteor jet had been proven in action and the speed of sound had become the yardstick of aircraft performance.

British society, too, changed beyond recognition during his lifetime, as did much of the western world. His childhood years unfolded in the last decade of Victoria's reign, an era when the country's military and industrial strength provided the foundation for an unquestioned, almost arrogant, national self-assurance.

By the time he died, the staid certainties which characterised Britain at the end of the nineteenth century had been overturned by two world wars and by dramatic social change. The complacent society of his youth, confident in the power of the world's greatest fleet and in the eternal nature of the vast areas of red on the world's maps, had given place to the Welfare State and the disappearance of empire.

The two global conflicts between them were the greatest catalyst for these decades of breathtaking change. The loss of so many of Britain's finest men in 1914-1918 had a catastrophic impact on the nation. In 1939-1945 the needs of increasingly technical global warfare changed for good the old concepts of 'the officer class' and of the immutable structure of society.

The military aspects of this age of change were nowhere more evident than in aviation. Only forty years separated the Wright Brothers from the jet age. Reggie Marix played a leading part as this drama in the air unfolded. He carried out the first successful bombing raid on Germany when he attacked a Zeppelin on the ground in Dusseldorf just two months after the beginning of World War One. During the twenty years of uncertain peace which followed 1918 he grew with the newborn Royal Air Force, despite the almost disabling injuries he received in a 1916 air crash. In the 1939-45 war, as a senior officer in Coastal Command, he flew in the lead Hudson in a devastating low level attack on German shipping in the Norwegian port of Aalesund. Later, based in Canada, he was the driving force in the complex operation which ferried huge numbers of American-built aircraft across the Atlantic to the Allies in Britain.

Behind the outward achievements of this skilled aviator and highly successful officer lay a very unusual personality. Born and brought up in turn-of-the-century England, with its rigid social code and harsh disciplines, he emerged as a man of sensitivity and charm, a charm which could be almost mesmeric to men and women alike. His ability to focus on the person with whom he was conversing was uncanny, in spite of – or perhaps even because of – the pain which was his constant companion after his First World War injuries.

A man of charm, certainly, but not the empty charm of the hail-fellow-well-met variety. His own values – old-fashioned things like honour, chivalry, generosity – were far too deep in him to permit of superficiality. Whether flying his tiny Sopwith over a hostile Germany in 1914 or speaking in French to a Quebec university audience, the intensity and concentration that he brought to the task at hand ensured that it was done well.

Air Vice Marshal Marix was a man who was fully the equal of any in the gallant band of RAF brothers as a pilot, as an officer, as a multi-faceted personality, and as a gentleman. The story in this book is of a life well lived.

Chapter One

The Early Years

1889. A great time to be born. Queen Victoria, full of years and glory, although still grieving for her beloved Albert, is entering the final decade of her reign. Her country revels in being the most powerful on earth. The officers of the Royal Navy know that their fleet is the strongest afloat. Great splashes of red colour the maps of the globe. God's in His heaven, all's right with the world.

A feeling of self-confidence, perhaps even of smugness, pervades the upper strata of society. The practice of religion is widespread, if not universal. The Law and its enforcement are strong. On the surface, at least, Britain's is an ordered society at the peak of its powers. People see no reason why that peak should not remain as a plateau. *Pax Britannica*, in a word, is here to stay.

The lives of the submerged underprivileged, however, are very different. For them, the struggle is to climb out of the Dickensian depths of poverty and ignorance to which the Industrial Revolution has condemned them. Grinding factory work, poor education, inadequate food, insanitary housing are still their lot. As late as the year before the First World War, Geoffrey Marcus notes in *Before the Lamps Went Out*: "'What do I care for the Empire on which the sun never sets?" exclaimed a daughter of the slums. "Down our court the sun never rises!"'"

Beneath the self-satisfied and placid surface of the late Victorian England lurks social and political turbulence which will shape the next century. Only three years later, Keir Hardie becomes the first Independent Socialist MP. Twenty years of upheaval are to pass before women are enfranchised. Future changes in sexual mores will reveal the Victorian ethic as having been infused with hypocrisy.

Abroad too, change is in the air. The United States, Germany and Japan are all growing powers who will challenge British economic or military leadership. The 1881 Boer War is a precursor of bigger movements in South Africa. Marxist inspired International Socialism is fermenting into the brew of full-blown Communism. Military developments (aviation, submarines, wireless) which will upset the balance of power are just over the horizon.

But all this sub-surface confusion doesn't disturb the placid calm of 17 August 1889, when James and Amy Marix become the proud parents of Reginald Lennox George.

★   ★   ★

James Marix came from an old Huguenot family. Split asunder by religious persecution over the centuries, it now had branches in England, Germany, and the United States. James spent long periods in America as a journalist for *The Times*, and in fact with the looser handling in that era of bureaucratic foibles like passports and immigration laws, he was probably taken as an American. He forged a strong link with the history of the US by having been in Ford's Theatre as a reporter for his newspaper when John Wilkes Booth assassinated President Lincoln in 1865.

Newspaperman, traveller, gambler (the erratic nature of his finances was due to his devotion to the horses and the tables) – Reginald's father was all of these. But most important of all, he was late Victorian man in full flower. Photographs of him taken around the turn of the century show him dressed formally in the manner of the day, but with a rakish air, modelled perhaps on the style of the future Edward VII. A man, in the words of T.S. Eliot, 'on whom assurance sits as a silk hat on a Bradford millionaire.' In that respect he was no different from his contemporaries in England of the time. Surface conformity and apparent rectitude sat easily with enjoyment of *la bonne vie*. We can conjecture little of his inner self; he is but a faint memory in the minds of those still alive.

Of the young Reggie's mother, we know less. Amy Powell came from Welsh stock, and appears to have had a strong personality. Certainly the sepia photographs of her reveal a very lovely lady, hidden though she is in the silks and bombazines of the time.

An interesting sidelight on the links in time and space provided by the family line is that Reggie's son, Nigel, has a clear childhood memory of his grandfather, an impressive man with an equally impressive beard. He remembers also, but with less clarity, the beauty of his grandmother. Nigel is the connection between the man who witnessed Lincoln's assassination and the Bush administration of the 1990s.

Such was the home into which the young Reggie was born. The Cromwell Road, in west London, now the route of traffic hurtling to and fro between Heathrow airport and the city, was their base. It was the London of Conan Doyle's Sherlock Holmes, of Oscar Wilde, Jack the Ripper, Gilbert & Sullivan. For the family – small for the time, with just two children, Reggie and his sister Rika – it was a time of financial ups and downs. Early photographs show the family enjoying the summer weather at fashionable seaside resorts – the south coast of England, or watering holes such as Deauville or Cannes. But the pictures don't reveal the occasions when the young Reggie's schooling was interrupted by his father's money difficulties, brought about by his flirtations with Lady Luck.

The impression is one of a loving family, with every care and expense lavished on the children – until the funds ran low, when things had to be cut back. The prevailing standard of the day in what would now be called 'child psychology' or 'parenting' was 'little children should be seen but not heard.' The formative years of the younger generation were not considered worthy of record until they had reached mature years, years of achievement. As a result, it is not easy to get a clear picture of the first several years of the future aviator's life.

★ ★ ★

Even of Reginald's school years, the record is sparse. He was at Upton School in 1904: a cup awarded as a prize for winning a 300 yard foot race exists as evidence. He went on to Radley College, where he spent just two years, from 1905 to 1906. The Archivist at Radley reports that he boxed at bantam weight, and that he was a rowing cox. Other than that, and the fact that shortly before the outbreak of the First World War he landed an aircraft on Radley playing field, little information exists.

It seems that his subsequent achievements in the war overshadowed his school record. Boxing and rowing faded into insignificance compared to aerial combat. But the achievements of his later life, and his charismatic personality must have had their origins in these early years of home and school.

After leaving Radley he went to the Sorbonne, where he matriculated in 1908. In Paris he became fluent in French, which was to be enormously useful to him during his career – he later qualified as a first class RAF interpreter in the language.

Still the record is thin. His time in Paris is not well documented. But it takes only a little imagination to envisage the fascination of that city for a young man of his age.

One exciting incident illustrates his sense of adventure. Somebody bet him that he wouldn't walk through the '*apache*' area of Montparnasse at midnight, wearing white tie and tails. The *apaches* were the often anarchistic, sometimes violent denizens of the back streets of Paris of that time. To stroll among them alone and unprotected was considered hazardous to the health.

But he took the bet. He must have believed in the invulnerability of youth, and in his jiu-jitsu skills. Wearing a top hat with his tails, apparently armed with only a silver-mounted ebony stick, every inch the English dandy, he walked unscathed from one end of the quartier to the other.

Superstitious by nature, the *apaches* must have decided that he was not dealing from a full deck and decided to leave him alone. The .32 automatic concealed under his tail coat was never called into play.

★   ★   ★

By 1909 Reggie Marix's formal academic education was over. He went to work with a 'well-known surveyor and estate agent in Chancery Lane.' But the routine predictability of a business career in the City of London was not in the long term going to suit his adventuresome energy.

On 20 May of that year, he enrolled in the London Division of the Royal Naval Volunteer Reserve. Perhaps he already had an inkling of what was ahead. Whatever his thoughts, he had begun laying the foundations of a service career which would continue until the church bells signalled the end of the Second World War.

Chapter Two

Naval Aviation: 1909–1914

Three things came together for the young Marix as war clouds, scarcely noticeable at first, gathered over Europe.

First was his naturally adventurous spirit, the nerve that had propelled him among the *apaches* of Paris. This sense of daring, in the context of an all-powerful maritime England, led the nineteen year old naturally into an armed service career.

Second was the thrill of the new technique: flying. In December 1903 Orville Wright made his historic forty-yard first powered flight. Two years later, the brothers flew twenty-four miles. In 1908 they brought their aircraft to Europe, pioneering powered flight in Britain, France, and Italy. The following year, Reginald Marix put the letters RNVR after his name. This was just two months before Bleriot flew the English Channel, awakening British and German military interest in aviation.

The third factor was the imminence of war itself. It is hard to say if at his age he was specifically aware of the growing alliances which were girding for war. Certainly with his intelligence and awareness he would have known that Great Britain and its empire were to be put to the test. As part of the generation which responded to the 1914 call to arms with enthusiasm, he probably thought with Rupert Brooke:

> Now, God be thanked Who has matched us with His hour,
> And caught our youth, and wakened us from sleeping . . .

Adventure, aviation, and the distant bugles were the three forces acting upon Marix when he was deciding the future course of his life.

★ ★ ★

His Record of Service from Sub Lieutenant, Royal Naval Reserve in 1912 to Air Vice Marshal in the Second World War is preceded by an entry under the heading 'Previous Service'. 20 May, 1909, it states that Reginald Lennox George Marix was enrolled in the Royal Naval Volunteer Reserve. The entry under that heading concludes with: 'Discharged as Leading Seaman on appointment to a commission November 01 1912'.

This refers to his time in the London Division of the RNVR when he was a business denizen of Chancery Lane. Maybe he saw that service as personal preparation for the war which was becoming progressively more certain; or perhaps as just an outlet for his enterprising nature. Evening lectures, weekend sailing, naval training, all led him into his life's career.

His service must have made him keenly aware of the inevitability of the maritime use of aircraft. Vice Admiral Sir Arthur Hezlet, in his 1970 book *Aircraft and Sea Power*, comments: 'The period 1910-1911, therefore, was one in which the principal navies of the world began to take to the air . . .'

Apart from his sense of the probability of a European conflict and his natural attraction to aviation, the London Division of the RNVR was a fine club to belong to. It had only been formed a few years previously, in 1903, with the Hon. Rupert E.C. Lee Guiness, CB, CMG, in command, originally headquartered in HMS *President* in the West India Docks. In the true spirit of volunteerism, it was run on a shoestring: a brief history of the RNVR points out 'a capitation grant of 55s. per annum was paid to the divisions from Admiralty funds for each efficiency rating on the books. This was insufficient for running the division, and the commanding officer had either to put his hand in his pocket or raise funds locally by means of public subscriptions.'

The Head of the Naval Historical Branch writes '. . . the Lower Deck of the pre-WW1 RNVR had a bourgeois flavour – the sheer cost of the uniform and kit was more than the average working man could afford to fork out for a pastime, however patriotic.' So Reggie Marix belonged, in those few pre-war years, to what was in effect a club with a high degree of exclusivity; a club, however, that combined social standing with a solid core of training in the ways of the Navy.

It was clear to Marix, RNVR, that he was at precisely the right moment to combine flying with Navy, and to be in on the ground floor of an entirely new military development – aviation. On 17 June 1912, Petty Officer First Class Marix wrote from 54 Norfolk Square, Hyde Park, to his commanding officer, Lieutenant Leander McCormick-Goodhart, who lived not far away at 73 Eaton Terrace. His letter was an application to join the Naval Wing of the Royal Flying Corps.

His request was forwarded to the Admiralty Volunteer Committee by Commander Guiness. On 1 November 1912 he was commissioned as a Sub Lieutenant in the Royal Naval Reserve (all non-RN officers in the RNAS held Reserve ranks), and posted to the Royal Flying Corps Naval Wing, HMS *Actaeon*. Two weeks later on the 16th, off he went to Eastchurch, on the Isle of Sheppey.

Eastchurch had been set up only the year before with the very reluctant acquiescence of their Lordships as the first naval flying school. The humiliating wreck of Naval Airship Number One, the *Mayfly*, in 1911, had hardened the hearts of the 'nautical faction' (Sir Arthur Wilson, for example, First Sea Lord, and Admiral Sturdee) against the new air dimension. Sturdee, on seeing the wreckage of the unfortunate airship, is reputed to have declared, 'It is the work of a lunatic', thus summarising the official attitude to flying.

There was therefore an antipathy to the concept of naval aviation on the part of the salty traditionalists. But a philanthropist, Mr Francis McLean, had persuaded the Admiralty to allow four officers to learn to fly, at his own expense. This was an offer they could hardly refuse. By the end of 1911 the new school's equipment had grown to six machines, and it had trained ten pilots.

Hugh Popham, in *Into Wind*, notes that '. . . in 1912 Winston Churchill was learning to fly with the first handful of naval pilots at Eastchurch . . . George Cockburn taught its first four officers to fly in the chilly April of 1911 . . . Eastchurch became the first Royal Naval Air Station, and the nursery of naval aviation.'

On 1 December 1912, after two weeks at Eastchurch he was sent to the Bristol School, where on 21 January 1913 he was awarded his Royal Aero Club certificate 'taken on Bristol Biplane at the Bristol School, Larkhill, Salisbury Plain.'

Military flying training today is an elaborate process taking years to progress from basic training to piloting an aircraft in a jet fighter squadron. Computer-driven simulators supplement unending hours in the air. Trainees require a high entry level of physics and mathematics to handle flight theory and aerodynamics, and so avoid wasting time on background education. Highly qualified instructors fly with the trainee until certain of his competence to go solo. Only after the most rigorous tests of ability is the new pilot let loose on one of the unbelievably costly jet aircraft of today.

Marix's training was of a very different nature. When the Royal Aero Club issued his certificate, only nine years had passed since the Wright Brothers' first hesitant flight at Kill Devil Hill. Aeronautics had not yet developed into a sophisticated science. Most importantly for the trainee, the low engine power and small size of their machines meant that they could only lift one person into the air. One either went solo, or not at all!

On the ground, the instructor would give on-the-job training perched behind the single seat. When he felt that his student had more or less got the general idea he would jump off the fuselage and clap the trainee's shoulder as a signal to take off.

This hit or miss 'training programme' produced as many failures as successes. A failure unfortunately seldom came back to tell of the reasons for the crash. Only the successful could add to the body of knowledge to help the next trainee. Statistics are hard to come by, but an educated guess is that as many or more young pilots were lost to training accidents as were claimed by enemy action. Marix was among the fortunate élite to survive the rough and ready flying instruction of his time.

On 17 January 1913, with the winds of war gathering force, he was posted to the Central Flying School at Upavon. Here he found himself on Course No 2, one among nearly forty RFC pilots under training. The course Adjutant was an over-age Major by the name of Trenchard, who had been a trainee on Course No. 1. Trenchard, according to Susanne Everett in *Wars of the Twentieth Century*, 'learned to fly because the new skill seemed to offer the only break in a thoroughly undistinguished career.'

Undistinguished or not, Trenchard was promoted in 1915 to Major General, and became head of the Royal Flying Corps. Sir Hugh Trenchard was instrumental in creating the RAF, from the Royal Flying Corps and the Royal Naval Air Service, in April 1918, thus earning the sobriquet 'Father of the Royal Air Force.'

Father of the nascent service he may have been, but Trenchard's opinion of Marix subsequently became less than parental. In apparent disregard of Reggie's outstanding war flying record, Trenchard's adverse reaction was to be detrimental to the junior officer's career for many inter-war years.

The quality of parenting provided by Trenchard did not go unchallenged. A.J.P. Taylor in *English History 1914-1945* says of the highly ambitious ex-cavalry officer: '. . . he insisted that victory by air power alone was theoretically possible, and he riveted this doctrine on the RAF after the war. This was probably the most permanent, certainly the most disastrous, legacy of the First World War.' Further on in his book, Taylor continues: 'Trenchard, who was chief of the air staff for ten years (from 1919 to 1929), set his stamp on British air policy right up to the outbreak of the Second World War. Bombing, he held, could win a war all by itself; it was also the only means of not being bombed by others. Trenchard and his successors persistently neglected air defence.'

Again, making an unfavourable comparison with World War Two's Dowding: 'Perhaps it was no accident that Dowding almost alone among commanders of the RAF had started his career as a gunner. Nearly all the rest, from Trenchard onwards, had been cavalry officers, and their strategy was the last charge of the Light Brigade.'

Whatever the verdict of history, it all adds strong emphasis to the point that Sub Lieutenant R.L.G. Marix, RNR, was very much one of the founding members of the military aviation club.

On graduating from the Central Flying School, Reggie Marix returned on 17 April 1913 to Eastchurch. He was cast in the role of instructor, with the rank of Flying Officer, Royal Flying Corps, Naval Wing. Or rather, a dual rank: he also carried the rank of Lieutenant RNR. Officers in the Naval Wing of the RFC before 1 July 1914, when the RFC and the RNAS officially became separate entities, and in the RNAS after that date, were distinguished by having two ranks.

In July 1914 he thus became a Flight Lieutenant, RNAS, while retaining his two stripes as a Lieutenant, RNR. After the war had started, the 'Reserve' part of his rank seemed to fade away, perhaps because, unlike most RNAS officers who had temporary rank, he enjoyed a permanent commission in the RN Air Service.

These constant changes of rank and title were a reflection of the fact that at that stage of development aviators were neither fish nor fowl nor good red herring. They were seen as an adjunct to the army – artillery spotters, observers. They had some possible role at sea. Trenchard was determined that they would become an independent force. That explains why, in his first seven years as an officer, Marix had no less than eight different ranks.

James Marix, financier and journalist. 'In the city'.

Reggie, a seaside holiday in France.

Reggie and his mother on holiday.

Reggie and his sister, Rika.

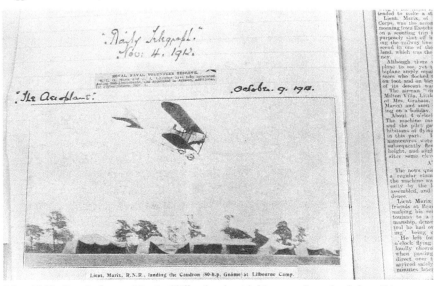

May 1913, Reggie flew to King's Cliff to lunch with his aunt. Later landed on Frinton Golf Links and had tea with his sister!

Reggie 1914.

Chapter Three

1914: War

On 3 August 1914 the British Foreign Secretary, Sir Edward Grey, made 'the remark that has since epitomized the hour', as Barbara Tuchman puts it in *The Guns of August*: 'The lamps are going out all over Europe; we shall not see them lit again in our lifetime.' The following day, Britain and Germany were at war.

Reggie Marix was at Eastchurch at that fateful time, but six days later he was transferred to Scapa Flow on Fleet reconnaissance work. Not for long; the record reveals that on 1 September 1914 his posting was 'Antwerp, Bomb dropping Squadron.' This was the Eastchurch Wing, the Naval Wing of the Royal Flying Corps, commanded by the legendary Charles Samson, then Commander, later to be Air Commodore Charles Rumney Samson, CMG, DSO, AFC, RAF.

Antwerp was strategically placed to challenge the potential Zeppelin menace. The bomber aircraft was still only a concept, but at least the Belgian city put the machines of the day almost in range of the airship bases at Cologne and Dusseldorf.

Count Ferdinand von Zeppelin, by this time 76 years old, had been the driving force in the development of the rigid airship which bore his name. As early as 1908 one of his craft made a twelve hour flight over Switzerland, which greatly impressed the Count's fellow countrymen. A year later, he formed the first passenger air-travel company in the world,

17

which in five years flew 100,000 miles with not a single casualty.

These achievements had not gone unnoticed by the British. The potential of the Zeppelin to carry troops and bombs to attack the country was evident, and countering technology and tactics were uncertain. It flew high, by the standards of the day; it had much greater range than heavier-than-air machines; its payload was substantial. Military planners therefore saw the Zeppelin as a major threat, a dagger at the throat of a virtually unprotected Britain.

Germany entered the war with some thirty of these monstrous machines – from five to eight hundred feet long, filled with up to two million cubic feet of highly combustible hydrogen. In theory they should have been easy targets for contemporary fighter aircraft, rudimentary though they were. In practice, their ability to fly at high altitudes and the inadequacies of fighter gun ammunition proved to offer them a degree of invulnerability in the early stages of the war. It was not until June 1915 that Flight Sub-Lieutenant Warneford earned his VC by dropping six bombs on a Zeppelin flying over Belgium at six thousand feet – a daring and successful exploit, but one in which his aircraft was thrown out of control by the explosion.

Early assessments were therefore that the Zeppelins would be at their most vulnerable on the ground, and it became a priority objective to destroy them there. It had to be done quickly if this menace to Britain were to be averted. There was a sense of urgency to attack the enemy's airships in their sheds while there was yet time, before the invading German tide could sweep away the machines which could do the job.

That invading tide was running fast against the Allies. German General Count von Schlieffen, who had died the year before the war began, had spent his retirement years working on a grand operational strategy for a war between Germany on the one hand, Russia, France and Britain on the other . . . the Schlieffen Plan. An essential element of his plan was to outflank the strong French fortifications facing Germany by a scythe-like attack through Holland, Belgium and Luxembourg – ignoring the neutrality of those countries.

The Schlieffen Plan meant that Antwerp would be scheduled for capture early in the war. But Antwerp was one of the very few places, perhaps the *only* place, from which the Zeppelin sheds at Cologne and Dusseldorf could be attacked by aircraft. The machines of the day were of course slow (ninety miles per hour was a good speed) and of very short range, so the inevitable loss of the city would ensure the safety of the German airships in their sheds.

Samson's handful of keen-as-mustard flyers with their motley collection of ill-assorted machines had their work cut out to destroy those airships in the little time left to them. To attack the Zeppelin bases while Antwerp was still tenable became their overriding goal.

★   ★   ★

Samson's Eastchurch Wing had arrived in Ostend at the outbreak of war. The first assignment was to cover the exposed left flank of the Allied armies against the German thrust, using their aircraft and armoured cars. Among Samson's ten pilots were Bell Davies, Bigsworth, Collet, Spenser Grey, and of course Reggie Marix. They 'brought a tremendous zest and a completely unorthodox, but most historical, appetite for private adventure' wrote Hugh Popham. 'They were like privateers operating under Letters of Marque.'

Within a few weeks this covering operation gave way to the more urgent task of countering the Zeppelins. At first the squadron didn't have much luck. The machines were so slow, so short ranged, so lacking in instrumentation that the slightest worsening in the weather could abort an operation. In *Fights and Flights*, Samson describes one such:

> 'On 22 September the long-expected attack was made on the Zeppelin sheds. Four aeroplanes started out from Antwerp, flown by Major Gerrard, Lieutenant Collet, Lieutenant Marix, and Lieutenant Spenser Grey, the latter carrying Lieutenant Newton Clare as passenger. They started soon after daylight. The weather was very suitable at first but they ran into a fog at the River Boer, which extended as far as the Rhine.
>
> 'Collet was the only one who located his objective, and he made a splendidly determined attack on the Zeppelin sheds at Dusseldorf. Unfortunately, he was too low for his bombs to function, as at his low altitude combined with the height of the shed sufficient time was not permitted for the safety fan of the bombs to unwind, thus preventing the explosion of the bomb when it hit. One of the three bombs that missed the shed exploded just outside the door and killed two or three soldiers.'

Although the four aircraft returned safely from this mission, it could not be termed a howling success. It would be another couple of weeks before Reggie Marix would be able to claim a victory, the first successful bombing raid of the war on German territory.

During those two weeks the German advance made the fall of Antwerp imminent – and with its fall would go the last chance of having a crack at the Dusseldorf and Cologne bases. The decision to evacuate the city was made, but Samson left two aircraft and a handful of mechanics to take this last chance. The two pilots were Squadron Commander Spenser Grey, in command of the tiny force, and Flight Lieutenant Marix.

8 October found the city within easy range of German artillery. On the previous night, the two pilots left their machines out in the middle of the aerodrome, where they felt that there was less chance of their being damaged by shellfire.

Samson tells the bare bones of the story that followed:

'. . . Spenser Grey and Marix set off in their "Tabloids".

'Spenser Grey got to Cologne, but found it obscured by mist, and he could not locate the Zeppelin sheds; he therefore dropped his bombs at the railway station. He got back to Antwerp at 4.45 p.m. At 8.30 p.m. the enemy commenced shelling the aerodrome, and the two aeroplanes, his own and Sippe's, were both put out of action by shells. It was therefore useless to remain any longer, and he started off with the mechanics in a motor-car for Ostend.

'Marix, who had Dusseldorf for his objective, achieved a great success. He let go his bombs from 600 feet and scored direct hits with both of them; he had the gratification of seeing the roof fall in and flames shoot up into the sky, proving that he had destroyed the Zeppelin.

'He encountered a very heavy fire from machine guns, and his aeroplane was hit in numerous places; 20 miles short of Antwerp, close to the Dutch frontier, he was forced to alight owing to running out of petrol. Abandoning his aeroplane, he got into Antwerp after a most adventurous journey, going some of the way by bicycle and some by a railway engine. He got away from Antwerp in the motor-car.

'We were all very pleased at Marix's success, and he and Spenser Grey richly deserved the DSOs they were awarded. Thus the Squadron now possessed four DSOs after six weeks' fighting. Not bad going for a small unit.'

Chapter Four

The Dusseldorf Raid: Reggie's Own Story

Reggie Marix had an unusual talent for recounting a story. In later life, he would use his writing skills in musical criticism, in humour, in playwriting. Fortunately, he took the time to set down on paper the definitive version of what led up to the Dusseldorf raid, and what happened in those autumnal skies over Germany.

Most importantly, he gave an insight into the urgency placed at the highest level on containing the Zeppelin menace. It was one of those rare occasions when those concerned with national decision making in time of war bring the front line soldier (or – in this case – aviator) into their confidence.

In his own words . . .

As far as I was concerned it started with a telephone call from the Admiralty. I had recently returned from Scapa Flow where I had been flying reconnaissances for the Fleet, and on this particular morning late in August 1914 I was in one of the hangars at Eastchurch helping to dismantle a Gnome engine. I was told that I was wanted on the telephone. It was Squadron Commander D.A. Spenser Grey who had been Winston Churchill's pilot before the war and who had given him flying lessons.

He said he was with Churchill (then First Lord) and that I was to come to Admiralty House (part of the Admiralty which is the First Lord's residence) as soon as possible. I remember that my hands were black with oil – and castor oil at that – but the station staff cars were open ones, and the old road from Eastchurch to London was very dusty in the summer, so that in any case I would need a good wash on arrival. I decided not to waste time, and left as I was.

On arrival I was obviously expected, and in my even dirtier condition was shown straight into a small dining room where at a round table three men had just finished lunch. They were Churchill, whom I had met a few times at Eastchurch before the war, Spenser Grey, and an old man with grizzled white hair, dressed in an old fashioned black frock coat but wearing what looked like a petty officer's indiarubber or celluloid collar and a narrow bright red tie.

W.C. greeted me, 'Ah, Marix, just in time for coffee and a brandy, sit down.' (A fourth place had been laid). Of course I had no lunch, and incidentally that was the first time I had ever drunk liqueur brandy from a balloon glass.

After the servant had left the room I found out the reason for my summons. W.C. was keen to have a crack at the Zeppelin sheds at Dusseldorf and Cologne, operating from Antwerp, but how was it to be done with the naval aircraft then available? W.C. then told us about two little aeroplanes going begging at Farnborough. They were land adaptations of the Sopwith Schneider Trophy seaplane which had won the last race at Monaco, but having wheels instead of floats they were even faster. They had been sent to Farnborough for trial by the R.F.C., but had been turned down as unsafe. Would S.G. and I like to try them? If we liked them we could have them.

Both S.G. and I were fans of the Sopwith products and we could not believe that the firm would turn out something which was radically wrong. We said that we would like to try them.

We then discussed how the raids could be carried out, and now and then the mysterious old man made some remark to which, I am afraid, I paid scant attention until W.C., to some rejoinder of mine, said 'Are you sure about that? Because as the First Sea Lord has just remarked . . .' With a shock I realized that a Flight Lieutenant had more or less ignored the great Lord Fisher and decided it was high time to put a 'Sir' into my answers.

After we had finished talking W.C. took us into the drawing room to meet Mrs Churchill, where I became even more conscious of my dirty hand when she offered me hers.

The next day S.G. and I went to Farnborough, where we were introduced to the little biplanes. We were solemnly warned (1) not to fly in level flight as they were unstable at top speed (having 80 hp Gnome rotary engines, these could not be throttled back) but to climb or glide; (2) not to leave the vicinity of the aerodrome as in the event of an engine failure they were impossible to land in a field.

S.G. and I had previously arranged that if we were satisfied with the aircraft we would crack right off to Eastchurch. We were to wave to each other after a few circuits. As far as I could make out there was nothing although certainly the machine was very light on the controls compared with any other aircraft I had ever flown. We waved, and that was the last Farnborough saw of the two 'Tabloids'.

A 'Bomb dropping Squadron' was then formed for Antwerp (to which I was posted on 1 September 1914) under the command of Major E.L. Gerrard, Royal Marines. The Squadron finally included Captain C.H. Collet, RMLI (Ft. Lt.) with an old Sopwith, Ft. Lt. Newton Clare with another old Sopwith, Ft. Lt. H.V. Sippe with a B.E. (Gerrard also had a B.E.)

Lord Carbery with a two-seater Sopwith Tabloid joined us, but not long after his arrival he crashed with the Prince de Lignes as his observer. He stalled coming in to land, and I think this machine was overloaded with a passenger. Carbery damaged a knee and had to be invalided home, and de Lignes broke an ankle. The aeroplane was a write-off. S.G. and I with our two new Tabloids completed the party.

As I have mentioned, these single seater Tabloids were Schneider racers with wheels and fitted with an 80 hp Gnome. They did 90 mph on the level and had warping wings (not ailerons). The range was about 200 miles.

At Eastchurch they were fitted with a simple bomb dropping gear, a rack under the fuselage to hold two 20 lb. Hale bombs. The bombs were released by pulling on two toggles connected by wires to the pins holding the bombs on the rack. There was no bomb sight. As soon as they were ready, S.G. had flown them to Wilryck (the aerodrome just outside Antwerp), refuelling at Dunkirk on the way.

At Wilryck the officers were quartered in a mansion almost on the edge of the aerodrome, and a small party of mechanics and ratings were billeted in the vicinity. We gathered as much intelligence as we could about the Zepp sheds, made plans, and in the meantime carried out reconnaissance for the Belgian Army, to which we were attached.

Dusseldorf is about 110 miles from Antwerp and Cologne about 120. It was clear that none of us could get to either place and back to Wilryck with the amount of fuel we carried. We had become chummy with the Belgian armoured car officers; their famous leader was Baron de Caters, who was a real fire eater. He hardly ever came back from raids into the open country without Uhlans' lances, swords, and helmets as trophies.

We arranged with him that when all was ready and the weather favourable he would take some armoured cars well to the west, I think about 50 or 60 miles, fix up a landing field, and have with him supplies of petrol and oil so that we could refuel on our way back. He would also have with him some of our mechanics. We carefully marked the chosen spot on our maps and ground signals were arranged.

The first attempt was made on 23 September. I do not remember who was detailed for where, but I was found for Cologne. All went well as far as the Meuse, but after crossing the river the weather began to thicken, and soon the ground was covered with 100% cloud. At 2,500 feet I was well above it.

When I calculated that I was nearing the Rhine, I came down to try and get under the cloud, but the first things I saw were tree-tops sticking out of thick mist and I pulled out just in time. I made a second attempt a little later but according to my altimeter the cloud or fog must have been down to the ground. The only thing to do was to turn back. The weather was still clear west of the Meuse, and I found the landing ground to which we all got back.

The only pilot to score any success was Captain Collet, whose target was Dusseldorf. Here the weather was clearer. He found a gap in the clouds, got down, found the airship shed but unfortunately missed it, his bombs exploding nearby. (One version was that he hit the shed, but that it was empty).

De Cater had done a grand job in establishing the landing ground, quite a hazardous undertaking since Germans were all over the place in those parts. However, all went well, and all the aircraft and cars got back to Antwerp.

For the next week the weather was unfavourable, and there were various delays. By the end of September the whole situation had deteriorated, and there seemed little likelihood that Antwerp could hold out. Also, with the general German advance, it was now impracticable for De Caters to provide an advance landing ground – without it, our aircraft could not get to the Rhine and back.

So Spenser Grey and I induced some Belgian mechanics to construct and fit an extra petrol tank into our aircraft. With it we should be able to do the job. But there was a maddening delay in getting the specially shaped tanks made and fitted. By the time all was ready and the weather was right, Antwerp was on its last legs.

This was on 8 October. Churchill had come to Antwerp, and was at British HQ in the Hotel St Antoine. On that morning, Spenser Grey went to HQ and told W.C. that we were ready to start. W.C. replied that it was now too late, Antwerp was to be evacuated that day, and the Germans might be in that night. We were all to get out of Wilryck as best we could, and that was that.

W.C. then retired to the w.c., but S.G. followed him, and through the closed door went on pleading, explaining that we would get back in time to get out. It seems that to get rid of him, W.C. gave his consent.

What with one thing and another, it was afternoon before we were airborne, S.G. bound for Cologne and I for Dusseldorf. I had a good trip and got to my destination's without incident. But the shed was not where I had expected to find it, and my map had been wrongly marked.

So I had to fly around a bit, which excited some interest. I was at 3,000 feet and some A.A. opened up, but well wide of the mark. I found the shed further away from the town than expected.

I closed, and as soon as I was sure of my target I put my nose down and dived with my engine still on. One would not normally do this as it puts an awful strain on the rotary Gnome as the revs go up. One usually switched off to come down, but then it took a certain amount of time for the engine to pick up again. I wanted no loitering near the ground.

The Gnome stood up, and when I was at about 500 feet I released the two bombs, one after the other, and began to pull out of the dive. I had kept my eyes fixed on the shed but I vividly remember the rapid points of flame as the ground machine guns opened up. I had been robbed of surprise by having to fly around looking for the shed.

Having got into a climb, I tried to turn away, but to my momentary consternation found that I could not move the rudder. The rudder bar was quite solid, and I was heading further into Germany. But I quickly appreciated that one can turn, although more slowly, on warp alone. This I did, and set a course for Antwerp.

As I pulled out of my dive I looked over my shoulder, and was rewarded with the sight of enormous sheets of flame pouring out of the shed. It was a magnificent sight.

The wind must have shifted, as I got some 5 to 10 miles north of my track. When I realized this, the light was beginning to fail and I knew I would have a job to get back to Wilryck before dark. Also I was getting worried about my petrol, and I simply dared not risk a forced landing with no rudder control. It was high time I got down.

I then had some difficulty locating a field big enough, as I needed more room without a rudder than with one. (By the way, I should have mentioned that the rudder was fortunately jammed dead fore and aft). I picked my field and got down.

Soon some gendarmes arrived and confirmed that I was north of Antwerp. I explained the situation, and the gendarmes helpfully said that shortly a railway engine would try to get into Antwerp to bring out a trainload of refugees, and that I could have a ride on the footplate.

We were near the station, and while waiting I examined the Tabloid. I had been lucky. The rudder bar was connected to the rudder by duplicate wires on either side running through tubular metal guides fixed to the uprights of the fuselage. On the port side on bullet had cut one wire, while another had hit one of the guides, welding the other wire to it. The elevator was operated by a pair of wires on either side to the control column. A bullet had cut one of these.

I was wearing a leather skull cap, but had taken my uniform cap with me by letting it hang against my back suspended by a string round my neck (so as to have it if I had to land and get out in a hurry – or even if taken prisoner). There was a bullet hole through the peak.

In all, there were about 30 bullet holes in the wings and fuselage. No serious damage, so I arranged for the gendarmes to mount a guard until I returned in the morning with mechanics and petrol. I did not know that I was to be escaping west long before daylight.

I boarded the engine, but it could only get to within about 5 miles of Antwerp. With some difficulty I commandeered a bicycle and pedalled off.

It was not quite dark. I found that I could not ride into the city because a bridge I had to cross was strongly blocked with barbed wire. With the help of a sentry I got on the outside of the bridge rail, and hung the bicycle on my back. (Difficult, but can be done with a man's bike). I manoeuvred myself across by putting my feet between the rail supports and hanging on to the rail.

Antwerp presented a strange sight. It seemed to be quite deserted, with houses on fire here and there. I pedalled to the Hotel St Antoine, which was also deserted except for an old caretaker. That morning it had been a hive of activity.

By now I was rather tired, so before going any further I persuaded the old caretaker to produce some wine and something to eat. Refreshed, I pedalled off, and in one of the big squares came across some Belgian soldiers who had a couple of cars. I prevailed upon them to drive me out to the aerodrome, which was deserted, so we went to the house alongside where we British officers were quartered.

Here, as I discovered later, I might have ended my career. During my absence much had happened. The few serviceable British and Belgian aeroplanes had been got away. S.G. had returned safely from Cologne where, unable to locate the Zepp hangar, he had dropped his two 20 lb. bombs on the railway station. Only he and Sippe (whose aircraft was unserviceable) were left in the house with half a dozen marines.

When we arrived at the house in complete darkness, the two Belgians who had accompanied me began talking to each other in Flemish. Sippe was at a window in a darkened room and was just about to open fire on whom he took for three Germans when I fortunately called out something in English.

It seems that I had returned just in time, as the small party were on the point of leaving before any real Germans arrived.

I eventually got away in a small lorry with a naval mechanic and a couple of Marines. The road west was a nightmare, crowded with refugees carrying or pushing in wheelbarrows, etc, such possessions as they had room for. There were old men and women, children, all sorts of animals, and the pace was a crawl. Broken down vehicles had to be ditched.

As we got further west, the traffic thinned and we got to Ghent an hour or so after daylight. There I managed to obtain a very welcome breakfast, and later went on to Ostend where I joined Commander Samson who was there with No. 3 Squadron and some armoured cars.

I never heard what happened to my little Tabloid.

★   ★   ★

That was his own story. As the Press of the time, and even some more official reports, offered contradictory details, it is fortunate that he took the time to keep the record straight.

There was a postscript. 'The Director of the RNAS (Captain Murray Sueter) sent me a copy of an Intelligence report which reads:

THE DIRECTOR OF THE AIR DEPARTMENT

Submitted

I beg to report that I have met Colonel Dobson, who has just got through from Berlin. He informs me that as the result of the last aeroplane raid on Dusseldorf and Cologne, our aviators destroyed a brand new Zeppelin which had just been moved into the shed, and also a 'Machinery Hall' (probably meaning a machine or erecting shop) alongside the Zeppelin shed.

He also informs me that the occurrence produced great consternation in Berlin, as they did not believe such a raid was possible for a British aviator.

As a result the Germans seized the English clerks at the American Embassy, believing that they had informed us.

(signed)   J. Richards, Lieut. RNVR
October 1914

Marix adds: 'I had received no information. It was just luck that a Zepp was in the shed.'

Chapter Five

After Dusseldorf

The impact of the successful raid on the Zeppelin base and the destruction of one of the latest German airships was dramatic. Europe had only been at war for a short time; the British public were surprised and elated to learn of this astounding feat in the air. In Germany, the idea of the Fatherland being attacked on its home turf was a difficult one to take in.

The concept of powered heavier-than-air flight was new. Even newer was its skilful and intrepid use against the enemy. The exploits of the Naval Wing of the Royal Flying Corps were splashed across all the popular journals. No aviator was more publicised than Reggie Marix.

Official recognition came quickly. *The London Gazette* of 23 October 1914:

> 'Flight Lieutenant Marix, acting under the orders of Squadron Commander Spenser Grey, carried out a successful attack on the Dusseldorf airship shed during the afternoon of the 8 October. From a height of 600 feet he dropped two bombs on the shed, and flames 500 feet high were seen within 30 seconds. The roof of the shed was also observed to collapse. Lieutenant Marix's machine was under heavy fire from rifles and mitrailleuses, and was five times hit while making the attack.'

In *The VC and the DSO*, Creagh and Humphries quote the *Gazette*, and go on to add 'for his services on this occasion, he was created a Companion of the Distinguished Service Order.'

The award was an early high point in his service career. Only two months into the war, the DSO came to him with this sonorously worded document from his King:

GEORGE R.

George the Fifth, by the Grace of God of the United Kingdom of Great Britain and Ireland, and of the British Dominions beyond the Seas, King, Defender of the Faith, Emperor of India, Sovereign of the Distinguished Service Order, to our Trusty and Well beloved Reginald Lennox George Marix Esquire, Flight Lieutenant in Our Royal Naval Air Service, Greeting

Whereas We have thought fit to Nominate and Appoint you to be a Member of Our Distinguished Service Order We do by these Presents Grant unto you the Dignity of a Companion of Our said Order, And we do hereby authorize you to Have, Hold and Enjoy the said Dignity as a Member of Our said Order, together with all and singular the Privileges thereunto belonging or appertaining.

Given at Our Court at St James's under Our Sign Manual this Twenty-first day of October 1914 in the Year of Our Reign.

By the Sovereign's Command

Kitchener

The Principal Secretary of State
having the Department of War
for the time being.

The King, although quick off the mark to recognize the officer and his achievement, had been preceded by the press. The *Daily Sketch* of 10 October 1914 featured a big photograph of **THE MAN WHO WRECKED THE ZEPPELIN** seated in the cockpit of his aircraft.

On the same day the more restrained *Daily Chronicle* ran multiple headlines for its story, in the manner of the time: **AIR WAR** was the top line, followed by SECOND VISIT TO THE RHINE. It went on: **ZEPPELIN SHIP DESTROYED; NEUTRAL POWER'S VIEW OF CAMPAIGN**. The paper's description of the raid was an abbreviated version of Reggie Marix's own. It added the comment 'the feat would appear to be in every respect remarkable having regard to the distance (over 100 miles) penetrated into country held by the enemy, and to the fact that a previous attack had put the enemy on their guard, and enabled them to mount anti-aircraft guns.'

The Call on 12 October featured a studio picture of Marix under the heading **DESTROYER OF KAISER'S ZEPPELIN AT DUSSELDORF**. But it was the *Sportsman* of that date which perhaps best caught public reaction. Under the headline **OUR HEROIC AIRMEN**, it ran:

'On Saturday the question in every mouth was, 'Who is Lieutenant Marix?' Of Commander Spenser Grey the public had already heard, for he was the airman who on occasions had piloted Mr Winston Churchill in aerial trips . . . but of Lieutenant Marix not even the initials were known . . . The fact that the outstanding achievements of the Flying Arm have so far been accomplished by comparatively unknown men clearly indicates that the Naval Air Service contains talent such as the public never imagined.'

The Times took a different tack, as one would expect from the Thunderer, then very much the newspaper of record. Under the headline **THE DUSSELDORF AIR RAID**, the subheading was **GERMAN ADMIRATION OF BRITISH DARING**. The story came from the paper's own correspondent in Copenhagen, and is worth quoting for its perspective from the other side.

'The latest British air raid into Germany appears to have caused some surprise in Germany . . . The *Rheinische Westfalische Zeitung* describes the successful attack on the airship shed at Dusseldorf. The flier was exposed to heavy shrapnel and rifle fire. Near the new shed he suddenly dived so that the spectators though he was hit. But he obviously dived to avoid the shrapnel and make more certain of his aim. With one shot he hit the shed about the middle of the roof. A gigantic burst of flame followed and there was great smoke for about 10 minutes. Externally nothing was to be seen but a large hole. It is supposed that the flier must have learned through treachery that this Zeppelin had only been transferred three days previously from the old shed.'

Many other newspapers carried the story, either as a piece of instant reportage or after the lapse of a few days as more in-depth analysis. *The Star*, *The Queen*, the *Daily Express*, the *Daily Mail* all covered the feat in their own ways.

Interestingly, the *New York Times* ran the story on 12 October, having received the news by cable. **GERMANS AT ANTWERP NEARLY POTTED MARIX** was the headline. It was sub-headed **BRITISH AVIATOR WHO DESTROYED DUSSELDORF ZEPPELIN ESCAPED WITH THE LOSS OF HIS MACHINE**. Reggie Marix's fame had quickly spread to the United States.

More deeply researched articles followed in popular and specialized magazines. *The Aeroplane* of 14 October contented itself with the brief story put out by the Admiralty's Official Press Bureau, but added a biographical sidelight on the pilot, illustrated with his photograph:

> 'Flight Lieutenant Marix was formerly in the Royal Naval Volunteer Reserve, and was appointed to the Royal Naval Air Service in its early days. He soon established a Service reputation as a skilful flier, and did excellent work on a Caudron biplane with the Naval detachment in the Army Manoeuvres of 1913. Early this year he looped the loop on the same machine. He has flown every make of aeroplane owned by the Navy, and seems equally skilful on all of them. He was educated at Radley, and his school may well be proud of him as the first British pilot to destroy an airship.'

Flight magazine of 16 October covered the story fairly briefly The writer differed from Reggie Marix's own account by saying that he had been picked up by a naval armoured car after abandoning his aircraft on the return trip. It added one other interesting titbit, a quote from the *North German Gazette* which represents an early attempt at disinformation:

> 'The airman's undertaking was only successful to a very slight extent. The Dusseldorf shed, which was constructed in the year 1910 and belongs to the town, is one of the most modern airship sheds, and was protected as far as is possible against attacks from the air. In the construction of airship sheds it was naturally necessary to take bombardment into account. Measures of precaution therefore were taken which cannot be discussed, but which, as the present case shows, are nevertheless effi-

cient enough to prevent the airships lying in the sheds from sustaining very serious damage. The airship which has just been damaged, and which had already gained some brilliant successes in the war, should be ready for active service again in a very short time.'

The writer of that piece was setting a precedent so well followed by Doctor Goebbels in the Second World War.

The Sphere came out on 24 October with a magnificent double page illustration showing the attacking dive of the Tabloid and the effect of the bomb on the airship shed. **THE BURNING OF THE NEW ZEPPELIN SHED AT DUSSELDORF** was the caption. The story was a shortened version, but contained an interesting observation: 'Since the visit of the aeroplane the nerves of Dusseldorf have been so badly shaken that the general in command has had to issue a communiqué rebuking the inhabitants and advising them not to become so agitated when the enemy score.'

★ ★ ★

Flight Lieutenant Marix's destruction of the new Z IX in its shed brought a new dimension to aerial warfare. His slow machine, short ranged and primitively equipped, had proved capable in the hands of a determined aviator of pressing home an attack on enemy territory. His 20 lb bombs were enough to ignite the huge volume of hydrogen filling the airship, even though he had no bombsight and only the most elementary bomb release gear. The tiny Sopwith had shown itself capable of absorbing all sorts of punishment.

Reggie Marix's flying skill, coolness under intense fire, and tenacity in reaching his target brought him immediately into the public eye. More than that, however: his exploit, first of its kind in World War 1, brought recognition that the power of this new technology would grow beyond any weapon of earlier warfare. Reggie's accomplishment helped start the chain of events which led to Bomber Harris's strategic bombing of Germany in World War II, and ultimately to Hiroshima and Nagasaki.

Even though the destruction of Z IX had demonstrated the power of aerial bombing, in the short term it was not able to halt the German programme to use the airship as a weapon of strategic bombardment. The storming success of the Schlieffen Plan, the fall of Antwerp, and the disappearance of any British aircraft within range of Germany put paid to repeat performances.

By the standards of the day, the German airship raids on Britain were terrifying and effective. In the course of the war, more than 200 Zeppelin flights unloaded nearly 6,000 bombs on the country, killing 522 people. British strategy had been rightly focused on elimination of this weapon as a high priority. It was only the speed of the German advance that thwarted the attempt.

Three years elapsed before the end of the airship bombardment. In 1917, strong air defence and bad weather broke up a mass raid over London. All the Zeppelins taking part were destroyed. The Germans attempted no more airship attacks on Britain.

★   ★   ★

On 28 October *The Illustrated War News* came out with a full page picture captioned **THE HERO OF THE AIR RAID ON DUSSELDORF ZEPPELINS: FLIGHT-LIEUTEN-ANT R L G MARIX AT OSTEND**. The photograph features what the text describes as an armoured car. It looks rather like an ordinary car with some plating awkwardly welded to it. That is probably what it was: Samson's team, forced out of

Antwerp and bereft of aircraft, saw their role as continuing to help the left wing of the allied armies by forming armoured car units.

The sailors trained as aviators were about to become soldiers.

★ ★ ★

In *Fights and Flights* Samson describes this phase of the war for his Squadron. Officers and men became adept at harassing the German units who were swarming through Belgium by this time. Many a successful ambush was carried out using armoured cars often hastily improvised from civilian vehicles and fitted with any weapons available. Tactics, too, were improvised. With the spur of combat they rapidly developed into highly effective manoeuvres.

Within a few days of his escape from capitulating Antwerp, Marix was in the thick of this new sort of fighting. These early days of the war saw cavalry used by both sides. The static horrors of trench warfare, the murderous defences of massed machine guns, the advent of the tank, were in the future. The Squadron operated in Flanders in mixed melées between its Heath Robinson armoured cars and German Uhlans with their horses and lances, ranging over miles of countryside not yet bogged down in the trenches.

Reggie Marix again showed his initiative and his ability to function under unorthodox conditions. Samson graphically describes an engagement:

'On 19 October we had some very tough fighting, and the 3-pounder proved its worth. Reporting to General Byng, he sent me on to General Kavanagh, one of the Brigadier's 3rd Cavalry Division, and from him I received orders to split up my party. One section, consisting of two armoured cars, was to attack

Ledeghem in support of some Cavalry, whilst the other
section, which comprised two armoured cars and the 3-
pounder lorry, was to support a Squadron of the 2nd
Life Guards, who were to deal with some Uhlans at
Rolleghemcappelle. I sent Osmond in Command of the
first section, and went myself with the second, taking
Marix, Warner and Lathbury. Staff-Surgeon Wells, with
an ambulance and a touring car, was in attendance on
both parties.

'. . . Marix, with his car, moved about 20 yards farther
up the road, where he got a good enfilade fire to bear on
another big body of Germans debouching from a wood
on our side of the village. This fire stopped them from
advancing, and they fell back.

'Marix arrived back at Poperinghe late that night,
having had a most interesting time. He had, after leaving
me at the windmill, gone back to Moorslede, and got
into Roulers, where he found the French Cavalry about
to retire. On the way back from there he found the
Duke of Roxburghe, who was severely wounded, lying
in a farmhouse with his servant standing by him. Marix
got him into the car, and thus saved him from certain
capture. Coming along to Moorslede via Passchendaele,
he arrived at the former place, where he found some
Cavalry outposts outside the village. I had just left, he
was told; at the request of a staff officer he did some
covering work with his Maxim on the Germans, who
were apparently about to advance through the town. In
this work he was assisted by a Belgian armoured car
driven by M. Charbon, a most gallant gentleman, who
well earned a reputation for his armoured-car work.'

These actions were the last of the mobile war. October/No-
vember 1914 saw von Falkenhayn and the Franco-British forces

locked in the bloody battle of First Ypres. The carnage became known as the 'graveyard of the old British Army.' It also resulted in the long drawn out trench stalemate which dominated almost the entire war.

Reggie Marix himself was involved in the fighting which led up to First Ypres, probably in the armoured car skirmishes which preceded the setpiece infantry battles. Later, he was stationed in Dunkirk, from where the Wing raided targets on the Belgian coast.

On 31 October 1914 he was promoted to Flight Commander, RNAS. If he ever had the time or the inclination to look back over the previous eight years, he must have pictured them as some sort of a whirlwind. Radley – the Sorbonne – the City of London – Royal Reserve – flying training – the Dusseldorf Zeppelin attack, and his well-earned DSO – armoured car and infantry fighting in the Flanders countryside – flying from the Dunkirk base.

But Reggie Marix thrived on excitement and challenge. He had no way of knowing what developments would call upon his fine-honed skills of combat flying. Whatever they were, he would welcome them.

As the winter of 1914-1915 dragged on, and the fighting men bogged down in the mud and blood of the trenches, the Allied leadership was searching for ways to break the deadlock. For Flight Commander Marix, DSO, there was more action to come.

Chapter Six

The Baron

Skirmishes against the rapidly advancing German units – many of them cavalry – kept Marix and all the other aviators of the Eastchurch Wing busy for the rest of that first year of war. Armoured car and infantry units intercepted the wide-ranging enemy patrols as they moved further into France and Belgium. These units bolstered the efforts of the allied armies to halt the Schlieffen Plan swing from the north-east.

To read the accounts of this stage in the conflict and of the part played by the fliers is a journey into a world lost for ever. 'High tech' and killing by remote control were developed in that dreadful conflict, refined in the Second World War, and 'perfected' in our own era. But at that time there was still an aura of sportsmanship, almost of civility. The age of chivalry had not yet totally expired.

Funeral services with full military honours were held for gallant and skilful enemy pilots shot down and killed over one's own territory. Fraternisation between British and German troops was widespread that first Christmas of the war, much to the consternation of senior officers on both sides. Warships routinely stopped to pick up survivors of vessels that they had just sunk.

No event underscores this continuation of an old code of chivalry more than a small but lively action in which Reggie Marix played the leading role.

In mid-October, Wing Commander Samson left him with a small group of troops guarding an aeroplane which had crash-landed near Ypres, and which risked capture by German patrols. This task was rather tedious to an officer of Reggie Marix's active disposition, so he set off in search of any Germans who might be around.

Taking with him eight soldiers and marines on this scouting expedition, he found quite a lot of them. German Uhlans were reported to be lurking in a nearby chateau; Marix surrounded it with his men. When they were all in place, he took two of them and advanced stealthily towards the old building.

With some two hundred yards to go, more than twenty Germans dashed out of the chateau, some on foot, others mounted. Reggie Marix and his team of two opened fire on the escapers. Their headlong rush indicated that they believed themselves to be opposed by a much bigger force.

The Germans who were already on horseback got clean away. But those cavalrymen who were on foot were not so lucky: their horses were behind a haystack, and the firefight turned into a running chase to see who would get there first. The British group won. One German was killed. The officer in command of the Uhlands and a trooper got to their horses, but too late.

Their horses shot from beneath them, the German captain decided that discretion was the better part of valour. He saw that Marix was taking aim at him, so he threw down his pistol, and handed over his sword as a sign of surrender. Reggie realised that the officer's horse was mortally wounded and was about to shoot it, when he thought that the captain might prefer to perform that sad task himself. He handed back the pistol on the German's word of honour that he would use it only to shoot the horse, the animal was put out of its misery, and the gun returned to Marix.

While this was going on, the German trooper accompanying his captain had been lying beside his horse – unhurt. Only after repeated orders from his officer did he get up and surrender his weapons – lance, sword, rifle and pistol.

Surrender completed, it dawned on the German officer that his party had been tricked into surrendering with so little fight. He found it hard to believe that the British force was one third the size of his . . . 'We thought you were the British army,' he complained angrily.

In *Fights and Flights* Samson describes Marix's delivery of the two prisoners, the Captain of Uhlans and the trooper, back to base and into the hands of the Provost-Marshal. The officer was still angry, but in Samson's words 'very punctilious.' His name turned out to be impressively fitting for a cavalry officer: Baron Wilhelm Freiherr von Lersner.

★   ★   ★

So ended a remarkable example of the chivalric afterglow that still hung over the mobile battlefields of 1914. Light forces, skirmishes between probing patrols, semi-improvised armoured cars versus brilliantly-uniformed cavalry: from our nuclear and electronic perspective the picture is akin to Arthurian legend. Not maudlin and sentimental, but civilised, gentlemanly and humanitarian.

Not quite the end of the affair, however. Through the rest of the war, and long after it, Reggie Marix had the Baron's sword in his keeping. He didn't look upon it as a prize of war, some emblem to reflect British versus German martial prowess. To him it was another's property to be held in trust until it was possible to return it.

The opportunity did not arise until December 1931, seventeen years after the event. By now a Wing Commander, Marix had spent time and effort trying to locate his old opponent among the chaos of post-war Germany. Not until all those years had elapsed did the Air Attaché at the British Embassy in Berlin finally pin down the Baron, by that stage working in a Berlin bank.

The sword was sent to the Attaché, who arranged a small ceremony to hand back the sword. This RAF officer then wrote to Marix to describe the occasion, as which in his own words 'all manner of pious sentiments for the friendship of the two nations were expressed.'

He went on to write: 'Von Lersner was a prisoner in France until very nearly the end of the War when he managed to get back to Germany by shamming lunacy. He is perfectly fit and well and an exceptionally nice man . . . he was really delighted to get (the sword) back.'

A post script was added by von Lersner himself in a letter of thanks for the return of the sword.

'I should like now to tell you personally how very much your magnanimous gesture has delighted me. Neither of us in October 1914 thought that the war would have lasted so long; and neither of us thought then that after the war so much distress would have pervaded the whole world and both our countries as a result of a misguided peace.

'The return of the sword just as this moment has not merely brought me personal joy, but I regard it also as a sign that the soldierly, chivalrous feeling, shown towards the opponents at the Front in the fight for existence, is purer and loftier than we otherwise experience in daily life or even in the political struggles among the nations. I should like to think that from those who fought in the war, irrespective of country, a new attitude of mind might develop which would lead to appreciation of the feelings and rights of others.'

The Baron went on to conclude 'I should be delighted to shake hands and thank you personally for your gracious gesture.'

Flowery words perhaps, but sincere and well-meant. Less than eight years after they were written, however, Europe was again engulfed in desperate conflict in which Reggie Marix was again to serve, this time at a much more senior level of command.

For the moment, he was happy to have played the gentleman even among the confused inhumanity of total war.

Chapter Seven

Gallipoli

By April 1915 the war had reached stalemate in the trenches. Attempts by both sides to break the deadlock – General Haig's at Neuve Chapelle, von Falkenhayn's response which led to Second Ypres – were destined to produce appallingly long casualty lists, but no breakthroughs. The Germans used gas for the first time during the months, but again to no avail.

The frustrated British leadership was in a mood to try anything, any change in strategy, to break through the ring of steel which the Central Powers had built around themselves. When beleaguered Russia pleaded to the western allies for a diversion to relieve the pressure on her from Turkey, she found willing supporters. The First Lord of the Admiralty, Winston Churchill, seconded by the First Sea Lord, Admiral Sir John Fisher (both of whom Marix had met during the discussion about the Dusseldorf raid) were already persuading the government that it would be feasible to force the Dardanelles and knock Turkey out of the war. The enemy, Churchill predicted, might well come tumbling down like a house of cards if this could be achieved. The impasse in France would be broken, and the war would be over.

The main assault on the Dardanelles took place on 25 April 1915, but naval landings had been ineffectually attempted in the preceding two months. Flight Commander Marix went out to this new war theatre with Commander Samson's No. 3 Wing, and was in the thick of the aerial operations during the landings at Cape Hellas, Anzac and Suvla Bay.

The flavour of Reggie Marix's part in this early example of ground support is best experienced through the eyes of Samson himself, in *Fights and Flights*:

'On May 2nd we had our first successful air flight, as an enemy seaplane came towards Tenedos. Marix set off in chase of him, and caught him up near Kephrez Point; he forced the seaplane to land on the water, and killed the observer. Marix came down to about 50 feet to do this, and of course got a hot time, as he ended up only about 300 yards from Chanak.

'On May 17th Marix had his big Breguet ready for action. As our principal objective with this aeroplane was an attack on Constantinople, we had to test it out well before allowing the attempt to be made, so in order to see what it could do I made one of my infrequent trips as passenger.

'We carried no less than one 100 lb. and fourteen 20 lb. bombs, and also a Lewis gun, a pretty formidable amount for those days. Off we set with the idea of giving Ak Bashi Liman a look-over. Arriving there, we found the place a scene of great activity. We let go all our bombs and created complete panic, and also did a lot of damage.

'I have since talked with Turks who were actually on the spot at the time, and they all said that we put a complete stop to work for two days, as the labourers fled to the hills. The loss of life was severe, thirteen killed and forty-four wounded.

'Marix and I came back delighted with the Breguet; but rather doubtful if the engine was reliable enough, as it was missing fire most of the time. However, we both had great faith in Dessoussois, who said he would get it right.

'During the first fortnight in June Marix was hard at work with the Breguet, making frequent flights to get it ready for the Constantinople trip. I went up three times with him, and on one occasion we got the bag of our life, as we found about 400 Turks in a gulley behind Anzac. They were in a dense mass, being paid or drawing rations or something like that. We dropped a 100 lb bomb at them, and following its flight the whole way with our eyes saw it burst immediately in the centre of them. We could see that the loss of life was tremendous.

'On June 21st Reggie Marix, with myself as passenger, set off at 1.30 a.m. for Constantinople. The engine started to misfire as soon as we left; but Reggie, a most persistent fellow, carried on. We got as far as Anafarta Saghir, which is beyond Anzac, when we both decided that it was hopeless to go on, so reluctantly we turned for home. On the way back we bombed every campfire we could see, and I hope disturbed the Turks a bit with the fourteen bombs we gave them. We neither of us thought we would reach Tenedos, as the engine went weaker and weaker and we came down gradually towards the water; we succeeded, however. Immediately we landed Dessoussois rushed up and started taking the plugs out. He got three out, then flung down his tools, and said, 'Commandant, what this pig of an engine wants is not a mechanician but one 'ammer.' He then burst into tears, and had to be led away. Pour soul, he had worked like a slave on the engine, although suffering from dysentery.

'Marix was terribly disappointed, as there was little doubt that the engine was a bad one; certainly if Dessoussois couldn't make it go nobody else could.

'Constantinople had to be given up. None of my other aeroplanes could carry sufficient fuel as well as bombs for this long journey.'

Such were the trials, tribulations, and successes of ground support operations in those technically primitive days. The aircraft were liable to all sorts of breakdown and failure, but the men flying them were a different breed. Samson again:

'Reggie Marix once bet me he could run to Tenedos, if I gave him five minutes' start, faster than I could ride on Nigger, the horse I had captured in France. Unknown to Marix I sent off one of my most expert Marines to clear away some of the principal obstacles, and to mark out the best bits of going, by whitewashed stones; then I accepted Reggie's challenge. He never had a dog's chance; I came close up to him before halfway. Pretending I was in difficulties, he was deceived into making fresh efforts; after a bit I had compassion and passed him, and we called the bet off. I am certain he would have broken a blood-vessel if I hadn't stopped him, as he was a most determined fellow.

'Marix was recalled to England in October. His departure was a great loss to the Squadron. Not only was he one of the finest pilots that there ever was; but he combined this skill with the most conspicuous gallantry and grim determination.

'If I told him off for a job, I knew the work would be done like clockwork. He never failed me once. I always considered Davies and Marix as the two most skilful pilots Eastchurch ever turned out. Reggie's departure made me feel that the old Squadron was beginning to break up . . .'

Reggie's part in the campaign did not go unrecognised. The Supplement to the *London Gazette* of Tuesday, 14 March, 1916:

Admiralty
The undermentioned Officers have been commended for service in action in despatches received from the Vice-Admiral Commanding the Eastern Mediterranean Squadron covering operations between the time of the landing on the Gallipoli Peninsula in April, 1915, and the evacuation in December, 1915 – January 1916.

The name of Flight Commander Reginald Lennox George Marix, DSO, RNAS, is in the list which follows.

The Dardanelles campaign was a failure – glorious, but a failure none the less. Names like Anzac and Gallipoli are woven into the history of the British Empire. Anzac Day is still one of the most nationally important days of the year in Australia and New Zealand, whose troops proved themselves in those terrible months to rank among the toughest fighters in the world.

Air support was insufficient to turn the tables in what turned out to be a wild throw of the military dice. But Samson's team in No. 3 Wing fought and flew to the limit of men and machines. Reggie Marix was on the cutting edge.

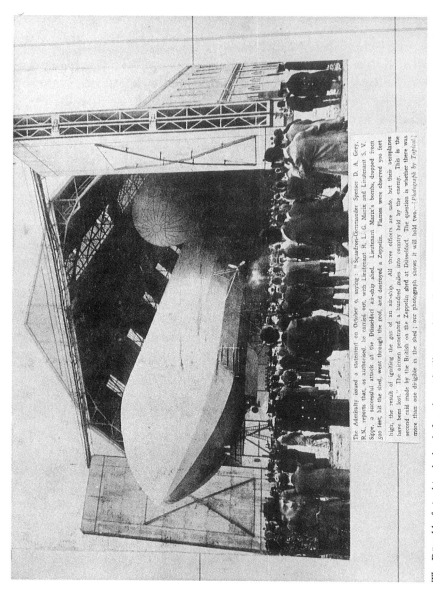

The Admiralty issued a statement on October 9, saying: "Squadron-Commander Spenser D. A. Grey, R.N. reports that, as authorised, he carried out, with Lieutenant R. L. G. Marix and Lieutenant S. V. Sippe, a successful attack at the Düsseldorf air-ship shed. Lieutenant Marix's bombs, dropped from 500 feet, hit the shed, went through the roof, and destroyed a Zeppelin. Flames were observed 500 feet high, the result of igniting the gas of an air-ship. All three officers are safe, but their aeroplanes have been lost." The airmen penetrated a hundred miles into country held by the enemy. This is the second raid made by the British on the Zeppelin shed at Düsseldorf. The question is whether there was more than one dirigible in the shed ; our photograph shows it will hold two.—[*Photograph by Topical*]

The Düsseldorf air-ship shed – before the raid. Illustrated London News 1914.

Reggie Marix, flying a Sopwith Tabloid, bombs the Luftschiff Z-1X, 8 October 1914.

HERO OF THE DÜSSELDORF RAID

'Daily Sketch' 10 October, 1914.

HERO OF THE AIR RAID ON DÜSSELDORF ZEPPELINS: FLIGHT-LIEUTENANT R. L. G. MARIX (TO THE LEFT, ON THE CAR) AT OSTEN
ently published Memorandum by the Director of the Admiralty Air Department it is stated: | The roof of the shed was also observed to collapse. Lieutenant Marix's machine was under heav
utenant Marix, acting under the orders of Squadron-Commander Spenser Grey, carried out a | from rifles and mitrailleuse and was fire times hit whilst making the attack.' Lieutenant Ma
tack on the Düsseldorf air-ship shed during the afternoon of October 8. From a height of | seen on the left-hand side of the photograph, standing on an armoured car outside the Headqu
dropped two bombs on the shed, and flames 500 feet high were seen within thirty seconds. | Hotel at Ostend. The photograph was taken on the day after his memorable exploit.

Ostend, Belgium October 1914 Reggie Marix, far left.

FIRING THE WASP'S NEST

The Spere, 24 October, 1914,

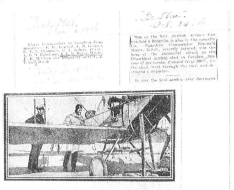

Mentioned in despatches, March 1916.

BRITISH NAVAL AIRMEN DISTINGUISHED IN THE WAR : OFFICERS OF THE NAVAL WING OF THE R.F.C, WITH THEIR MECHANICS.

Seated in the centre is Commander Samson, who has done excellent work in command of the Aeroplane and Armoured Motor Support of the Royal Naval Air Service. The Kaiser recently set a price of £2000 on the head of the Commander of the British armoured trains that have wrought such havoc among his troops, and it is generally assumed that Commander Samson is the officer in question. First and second on the left (of the officers seated) are Flight-Commander J. T. Babington and Squadron-Commander Briggs, who took part in the air-raid on Friedrichshafen. Fifth from the left is Flight-Lieutenant Marix, who raided Düsseldorf; and seventh from the left (with a white dog), Flight-Lieutenant C. F. Beevor, believed lost, while flying to France.—[*Photo. by Corbitt.*]

Officers of the Naval Wing of the R.F.C. with their mechanics. R. Marix, fifth from left – seated. Illustrated War News December 1914.

Pixie Marix. The Tatler.

Chapter Eight

Crash

Samson felt that 'the old Squadron' was beginning to break up, but Reggie's next appointment when he got back to England from the Dardanelles was to create a phoenix from the ashes. Following a brief spell at Eastchurch, he went to Detling to form the new No. 3 Wing. By April, he was commanding that Wing at Manston, in Kent.

Reggie's success over Dusseldorf had played a major part in convincing the country's military leadership that aircraft could be highly effective in the bombing role. Major Christopher Draper, DSC, in his book *The Mad Major*, sheds some interesting light on how this innovative thinking led to Marix's new job:

'. . . The earlier RNAS attacks on Friedrichshafen and Dusseldorf had evidently turned the Admiralty towards the idea of forming what must be regarded as the first strategic air force in the world. It might be as well to explain that the RNAS at this time did not have Squadrons in the same way that the RFC had. The service consisted of Naval Air Stations and Seaplane Bases, each of which might have anything from one to fifty aircraft. Right from the outbreak of war, however, smaller formations had been formed at these Stations and Bases, and were known as Wings.

'The beginnings of this strategic air force were to be found at Manston, near Margate, where 3 Wing RNAS was formed. It consisted at first of a miscellaneous collection of aircraft, which included a couple of Renault-engined BE2C's, an American Curtiss R2, a Short Bomber, three each of single and two-seater 1 Strutters and a machine described as a 'Sopwith School Bus.' A number of the Sopwiths which supplemented and eventually replaced these machines were erected at Detling and flown to Manston, then a virgin field with its personnel housed under canvas.

'The unit was commanded by Captain W.L. Elder, CMG, RN, who left for France with an advance party in May 1916, leaving Lieut. Commander R L Marix, my friend from Eastchurch, in command at Manston.'

(It is interesting that Draper uses the rank 'Lieut. Commander.' Reggie's Record of Service shows him as having been promoted to Squadron Commander, RNAS, on January 1 1916. There was always some difficulty in disentangling the RFC from the RNAS, not completely resolved until the formation of the Royal Air Force in 1918.)

In *Sailor in the Air*, Vice Admiral Richard Bell-Davies describes how he took over command of the newly-formed Wing from Reggie Marix, soon to be assigned the task of taking a squadron out to France:

'I . . . was appointed wing commander of No. 3 Wing about the middle of June. The squadrons were forming at Manston in Kent, where land had been taken over by the Admiralty and a few tents erected. The wing was to operate from Luxeuil, near the French frontier fortress of Belfort, where a large repair base was also to be set up, the whole organization under the command of Captain

Elder. At Manston I found Reggie Marix training the first flight which had just been formed. The pilots were nearly all Canadians and were a first-rate lot. The aircraft were to be Sopwith 1½-Strutters, which were just coming into production, and it was hoped that they would be followed by some twin-engined Handley Pages.

'. . . The 1½-Strutters were a great advance on anything we had had before. The bomber and fighter versions were in essentials identical aircraft . . . their operational range was excellent, and to test it Reggie had flown one from Manston to Mevagissey, in Cornwall, and back without landing.

'There was nothing much for me to do at Manston as Reggie had the training well in hand.'

By this time Squadron Commander Marix was a highly skilled pilot, capable of flying many of the types then in existence. He had as much combat experience as anyone then in the air, and had been decorated for his exploits. No officer was more suited to head up a fighting wing committed to using the new air weapon in support of the ground troops. Reggie's future was alive with promise. If he survived the hazards of the western front, he would be in the very forefront of military aviation.

It was not to be.

In October 1916 Reggie was severely injured in a flying accident. The French Nieuport he was piloting crashed shortly after take-off. Both his legs were pinioned under the engine; the surgeons managed to save one (at the insistence of his sister, who rushed out to join him) but the other had to be amputated.

There are two or three differing accounts of just how the accident happened. Draper:

'We flew out via Paris, landing at Villacoublay, but a ghastly accident spoiled my first visit to this enchanting city. Reggie Marix and I were motoring out to Villacoublay, and as we passed the aerodrome at Issy les Moulineaux we stopped to watch a Frenchman spinning a Nieuport biplane. It was the first time we had seen a spin and we had quite a discussion as to how it was done.

'When we got to Villacoublay I said I would like to try a spin and Reggie, who knew the local French aviators, borrowed a Nieuport for me. I found the spin quite thrilling but not difficult and managed both right and left-hand varieties. I don't known if my success tempted him or not, but off went Reggie in another Nieuport. When I landed I was surrounded by a number of French mechanics, gesticulating and shouting such a gabble of French that I could not grasp a single word. It transpired eventually that poor Reggie had spun into the ground and broken both legs. I felt partly responsible and was very sad.'

Bell-Davies:

'In July the first squadron of 1½-Strutters set out from Manston, led by Reggie. At Paris where they landed he was invited to try a new French machine in which he had a very bad crash and as a result one leg had to be amputated. The surgeons fortunately managed to save the other so that he lived to have a long career in the RAF; his loss was a grave blow to No 3. Wing.'

Bell-Davies had the date wrong by about three months.

Another version is that he had gone to Paris to collect a Nieuport with which to augment the number of machines in his Wing — at that time, the French were the biggest aircraft builders in Europe, and supplied many to the British services. He may have been using the fact that the RNAS had more 'pull' with the suppliers than the RFC had to get hold of a new machine!

When he arrived at the airfield, the Nieuport was there, but the French test pilot was nowhere to be seen. It should have been his responsibility to check the new aircraft thoroughly; the industry was still in its infancy, and the stringent manufacturing controls which characterized later times had not yet been introduced. The checking routines included a short test flight.

Reggie asked the airfield staff where he could find the test pilot. The rather sheepish answer was that, the hour being after eleven in the morning. *M. l'aviateur* had already departed for the local estaminet where he habitually took a few glasses of lunch-time wine. It was unlikely, M'sieu, that he would be back again before the next morning.

Reggie was not one to let grass grow under his wheels. 'Very well,' he said, 'I will test it myself.' And off he went into the October sky.

At about 200 feet altitude, one wing detached itself from the fuselage. The Nieuport, totally out of control, spun down like a wounded bird, and Marix was trapped underneath.

It is hard to be sure which description is closest to the truth after the lapse of so many years. For a pilot of his great experience and flair, it seems unlikely that he would put an aircraft into a situation from which it could not recover. On the other hand, for a defective machine to be delivered from the factory which was producing under the pressures of war is by no means inconceivable. It happened; and Britain lost the operational contributions of one of its finest airmen.

The press in Britain quickly picked up the news of Reggie's injury, and linked it with his earlier exploits. The *Daily Express*, for example:

'Squadron Commander Reginald L G Marix, DSO, RN, who is officially reported to have been severely injured, destroyed a Zeppelin in its shed at Dusseldorf in October 1914.'

There was great concern that an airman of his stature and success had effectively terminated his aviation career. But those expressing this concern had not taken into account Reggie's bulldog tenacity, which would not only enable him to continue his career, but to rise to Air rank nearly a quarter of a century later, in the Second World War.

The price he paid in life-long suffering will never be known. It could well have been a crushing blow to a lesser man, but for Reggie Marix it served to reinforce the core of steel which lay below the affable exterior. It would give him an ability to communicate with people, as though he used the interplay of personalities as a way of sublimating his own pain.

Handicapped? Obviously. Out of operational flying? Of course. No longer effectively in the war? Certainly.

Crushed? Defeated? Never.

Chapter Nine

From War to Peace

After his accident, Reggie knew that he would not fly again during the war. He began working on the painful hard work of once more becoming mobile. His right leg had been amputated leaving only just enough stump to enable the fitting of an artificial limb, and the left leg was severely damaged.

This enormous disability had more of an impact on him than on the average man. From the time when, as a young teenager, he had won a cup for running at Upton school until he showed his fierce determination in racing Samson, man against horse, during the Dardanelles campaign, his athletic prowess was an important part of his make-up. Wartime actions he had been involved in, such as the capture of Baron von Lersner, had needed his speeding feet to be successful. To lose that prowess had a profound psychological as well as physical effect.

The simplest, and perhaps the most obvious, course of action for him would have been to take his leave of the RNAS and return to his earlier existence in the City of London. After all, he was a decorated and well-known aviator. He had done enough – more than enough – for his country. He could retire from the fray with honour and graciousness. People like him were needed to go about Britain's normal business, even in time of total war.

But that was not Reggie's thinking. He was determined to continue his Service career, even though it would be a long time – if ever! – before he would again function as a pilot. He was inactive during the rest of the war, but by the time peace came on 11 November 1918 he was a permanent commissioned officer in the new Royal Air Force, which had been created only a few months earlier.

Between the time he had been so badly injured and the Armistice Day which ended the appalling slaughter in Europe, three events of major importance to him took place in Reggie's life.

On 10 September, 1917, he was awarded the *Croix de Chevalier de l'Ordre de la Couronne*, by King Albert of Belgium – a foreign order of knighthood. This was in recognition of his gallantry in the air and on land in the defence of the little country which had suffered so much.

It is odd, but not incomprehensible in the light of history, that Reggie's highest honour should have been from a foreign country and not from his own.

The second event was the creation of the Royal Air Force.

The Royal Flying Corps, with its Naval Wing, and later the Royal Naval Air Service had come into existence in a remarkably short time. Bleriot's first cross-Channel flight and the outbreak of war were only separated by five increasingly tense years, which gives some indication of the speed of development. At first, heavier-than-air craft were seen by many as an unimportant side-show in the military scheme of things. However, when their wartime effectiveness quickly became obvious, attitudes changed. As the war ground bloodily on, the official view leaned toward consolidating these new fighting machines into one military arm.

Suzanne Everett, in *Wars of the Twentieth Century*, notes:

'In April 1918 the British took the pioneer steps of uniting all their air units – the fighters and seaplanes of the Royal Naval Air Service and the fighters, bombers

and reconnaissance aircraft of the Royal Flying Corps –
into a Royal Air Force. Its first commander was General
Sir Hugh Trenchard ('Boom' to all his subordinates
because of his extraordinarily commanding voice).'

Vice Admiral Sir Arthur Hezlet KBE, CB, DSO, DSC, writes
in *Aircraft and Sea Power*:

'On 1st April 1918, the Royal Air Force had been
formed. At first this made very little difference and co-
operation went on as before. The Admiralty still
controlled operations and there was no change of policy
in areas which were purely maritime. Nevertheless all
operations were now joint between the Royal Navy and
the Royal Air Force to which latter service all aircraft
now belonged.'

Trenchard and Reggie Marix's future became intertwined in
this history-making time. Reggie was from this point on an
RAF officer, no longer a naval aviator. His allegiance would be
to the new Service, not to the Navy. Unfortunately, from the
very inception of the RAF, Reggie got on the wrong side of
General Trenchard, and stayed that way for many years.

The story is told of the big dinner party held to celebrate the
birth of the Royal Air Force, and the amalgamation of the
RNAS and the RFC. A great deal of champagne was con-
sumed, as could be imagined at an event of this sort, even in
wartime Britain. Reggie Marix, it is said, at the height of the
festivities managed to climb on the table, disregarding the
handicap of having just one leg. There he stood, the focus of all
eyes. Lifting his champagne glass high, he called out the toast
'Long live the Royal Naval Air Service!'

At the head of the table, Trenchard was understandably not
overjoyed to hear this acclamation for the superseded arm. He

asked, 'Who is that young officer, calling out "Royal Naval Air Service" at a time when we are concentrating on getting the Royal Air Force going?'

He was told that it was Reggie Marix. He had of course heard of the RNAS officer's exploits – who hadn't? – but he felt that this behaviour was most inappropriate on such an auspicious occasion. As a result, the new commander was less than enthusiastic about Squadron Leader Marix for many years. This antagonism held back his career progress until 1930, when Trenchard relinquished command of the RAF. He didn't actually retire, because a Marshal of the Royal Air Force, like an Admiral of the Fleet, is immune from retirement.

In fairness to Trenchard, it must be remembered that the new Service had to fight for its survival. The political manoeuvres bringing it into existence had barely scraped through parliament. In the 1920s it barely existed – every flier knew everyone else, and it was little more than an exotic and highly specialized club.

Against that background, Trenchard's sensitivity to actions or words by any officer hinting at regret for the passing of the RAF's antecedents can be understood. It remains a fact, however, that in spite of his gallantry and the service he rendered to his country in the first two years of the war, Marix received no promotion in the next decade.

There had been another source of potential antipathy between the two officers. It was rumoured that Reggie's fluency in the French language, and his familiarity with French customs dating back to his time at the Sorbonne, had put him in a privileged position with France's Minister of Aircraft Production. Thus favoured, the rumour went on, he was able to arrange preferential treatment for the RNAS in the matter of new aircraft allocations rather than for the RFC. France being the major European producer of aircraft at that time, this was an important advantage for him to gain for the senior service . . . if, of course, the rumour was true.

All things were taken into account – his disabled status, the weakening economic situation with its impact on the services, his ill-advised remarks at the dinner table, and the part he played in inter-service rivalry as far as aircraft procurement was concerned – the remarkable thing is not that he was not promoted, but that his outstanding abilities were regarded as justifying his retention as a commissioned officer in the new Service.

Finally in that momentous last year of war, Reggie met and married the girl who was to become his wife, and Nigel's mother. The daughter of Alice and Clifford Wadmore, landowners on the Isle of Wight, Violet Trevor Wadmore became one of the 'bright young things' who dominated Mayfair's *beau monde* in the 'twenties. Blonde and beautiful, she was the centre of attraction for young men wherever she went.

'Pixie' Wadmore was very young, perhaps ten years Reggie's junior. She fell for the injured war hero, his good looks, his strong personality. She seems to have been swept off her feet, even though the nature of his injury could have been expected to be to some extent repugnant to her. But then she was always attracted to the dashing, gallant type of man – the wealthy and often aristocratic drivers of the motor racing fraternity were among her favourites. In her eyes, Reggie measured up to these criteria.

The fact that he was older by a fairly wide margin may also have had something to do with the fascination he held for her. He probably had some of the attraction of an older brother or 'father figure'. Handsome appearance, a genuine war hero, enough age difference to imply maturity and authority, powerful personality – all these factors combined to ensure that Pixie would fall for the one-legged airman.

They were married in that last year of war. A year later, Nigel was born.

★   ★   ★

In 1916 Reggie had been a Squadron Commander RNAS, but in April 1918, as soon as the new Service had been launched, he exchanged this rank for that of Major. It was another year or more before the RAF created its own distinctive ranks, at which point he became Squadron Leader. His time was spent in the long task of recuperation, until he was appointed to a Headquarters post in December 1918. From then on, he became part of the pattern of a regular peacetime RAF officer for the next twenty years.

Two reflections on this period of his life, from his accident at Villacoublay until getting back into the mainstream of the new Royal Air Force.

First is the fact that he was kept on in the RAF at all. His record had been a remarkable one, to be sure, but the nature of his injury was such as to foreshadow a rather inactive role for him in the future. It is difficult to imagine a junior submarine officer, for example, or a captain of cavalry holding on to a commission after such a disablement.

But hold on he did. Through perseverance, certainly, and determination: the amount of self-discipline and conquest of pain to get himself back from hospital and into uniform can only be wondered at. He also used his very considerable charm and personality on the doctors in charge of his case, to get them to agree to recommend his retention in the Service. After all, they must have known that with one leg amputated just below the groin, the other one severely damaged, and with a future of continuous pain, he had in theory no business being in a military organization.

But all that personal self-control and ability to persuade would not in themselves have been enough. Trenchard's attitude notwithstanding, the powers-that-were must have been very convinced that Squadron Leader Marix was a most unusual man, one who would be of continuing and growing value to the infant Service even through the hard post-war economic days.

This conviction on the part of his superiors, combined with a lack of certainty about exactly what the future of aviation would need in terms of leadership, ensured that Reggie Marix would not end up on the ex-military scrap-heap that so dishonoured British governments of the 1920 s. It was a good decision.

The second reflection is on the crucial influence that his injury had on his life – not in the physical sense of no longer being a fine athlete, but psychologically, in his relationships with others.

He had always had an ability to make someone with whom he was having a conversation feel that he or she really *mattered*, that Reggie wasn't just talking out of politeness. This aspect of his personality was probably enhanced by the continuous pain he suffered; in effect, he used it as a way of 'getting out of himself'. The side effect was that while Reggie was talking to him, the other person felt that he was the most important person in the world. Reggie did not share in the egocentricity of the average human being. He used his extrovert nature to focus on someone else, and thus take his mind off his own hurt.

This trait was enormously impressive to the casual acquaintance, someone who might not know what he was going through, and who found this deep and sincere interest very flattering. There is no doubt that this characteristic contributed to the continuing success of his career.

★   ★   ★

The years of 1918 and 1919, as war gave way to peace, were thus momentous ones in Reggie Marix's life. He became a permanent officer in the newly-formed Royal Air Force; he married, and soon bore the additional title of 'father'; and he found for himself a permanent career, in spite of the effects of an air accident which might have discouraged a lesser man from further endeavour.

Chapter Ten

The Uncertain Peace

The war to end all wars brought no prosperity in peace. Europe was in physical and political turmoil. The economies of the combatants, except for the United States, were in tatters. The huge over-production of primary goods by overseas countries which had been demanded during the war years resulted in a stagnant market – they could no longer afford to buy the materials that European industry could produce. Unemployment became rampant: by June 1921 in Britain the figure exceeded two million. That was one of the worst years of depression since the industrial revolution.

Germany suffered the worst from this dislocation. A measure of its economic chaos is indicated by post-war inflation; at one stage in the 'twenties a pound sterling was the equivalent of nineteen million German marks. The country's disruption, and its perception of the terms of the Versailles treaty as having been viciously unfair, directly led to National Socialism, the revival of militarism, Adolf Hitler, and World War Two.

Reggie Marix's career during these two decades of uneasy peace has therefore to be set against the tumultuous backdrop of post World War One Europe. As an Air Force officer he could not be oblivious to the turbulence of the continent. He dedicated himself to being an effective part of Britain's defence in the times of further trial which lay ahead.

★   ★   ★

On 16 June 1920 Reggie left his headquarters job in England, and was sent to Germany, appointed to the Inter-Allied Armaments Control Commission 'for "T" duties in connection with seaplanes', as his Service Record formally terms it. Just three days later he was attached to the Prussian Naval Aircraft Sub Commission.

He served there for six months. At the end of that time, he went to Paris, attached to the IAACC there. After another six months, still with the Commission, he was off to Berlin, where he remained until October 1921.

A brief spell in command of a Motor Transport establishment, and then on 22 April 1922 he was appointed to Royal Air Force Depot, Inland Area 'supernumerary (non effective).' These were the words of officialdom – it is difficult to imagine Squadron Leader Marix as being 'ineffective' in any situation.

He remained there only until 25 September, when he took a course in Wireless Telegraphy (a new technique in aviation) at the RAF Electrical and Wireless School. From there he was appointed to the Air Ministry, to serve in the Chief of the Air Staff's Directorate of Operations.

After little more than a year, he specialised in Intelligence duties from 15 January 1924. Secrecy was of course the keynote of this assignment, and the details of his work there are difficult to discern through the fog of those post World War I years. It is safe to assume, however, that his language capabilities and acute mind fitted him perfectly for the task.

In October that year he was again appointed to the RAF Depot, Inland Area, and soon after that went on half pay for several months. Half pay was a reflection of the economic stringency of the times. The war had caused such colossal disruption that everybody, from the highest to the lowest, was affected in one way or another.

Soon afterwards, things took a turn for the better. 24 September 1925, Reggie arrived in Malta for his first peacetime taste of service in the Mediterranean. He was appointed to Headquarters for Air Staff duties.

The island of Malta was then a vital military base. Smack in the middle of the Med, it was in a commanding position to influence events in North Africa, southern Europe, and the Near East. It had a geopolitical impact on the use of the Suez Canal, and on Turkey and the Soviet Union's warm-water ports. With Gibraltar dominating the choke point at the sea's western entrance, the country owning both strongholds was a decisive power in the whole area. Britain was that country.

Thus, Malta in the mid-twenties was an important place to be. No one could have forecast just how important – it would take the desperate battles against the Afrika Korps, and the fight for Malta's survival against constant air attack in the next war to demonstrate that.

★   ★   ★

A year before his first stint in Malta, an event took place which would affect both Reggie's personal life and his career.

In 1924, he and Pixie were divorced.

When Pixie had fallen for him just six years earlier, his 'hero' image was an integral part of the chemistry which attracted her to him. Even in marriage, however, the magnetism which emanated from men of similar mould still had an enormous influence on her. Among her admirers were Count Zborowski and Barney Barnato – the 'Bentley boys', dashing competitors at Brooklands in the days when racing drivers were wealthy and enthusiastic amateurs, not the professional technocrats of today. Louis Zborowski it was who persuaded her to break her ties with Reggie.

Her involvement with these and other great sporting figures of the time was a major factor in bringing about the end of the marriage. Compounding the situation was Reggie's overseas appointment, which gave her more freedom in the heady atmosphere of the roaring twenties. Also, Nigel had been sent off to a boarding kindergarten (as were the children of most serving officers in that era) in Sussex, so Pixie's liberty was complete.

The effect on Reggie was twofold. Outwardly, he continued to live the social life of an officer, first in Malta and then back home in England. He was a fine raconteur, and always in great demand: the attractiveness of his personality and his prowess at skills such as playing the piano and demonstrating his powers of hypnosis always ensured his popularity. Over the next many years, he was friendly with a number of beautiful and intelligent women, but during the whole of his remaining time in the RAF he did not remarry.

Inwardly, it was a different story. 'Once bitten, twice shy' is too trite a phrase to explain his reaction to the divorce. It went deep into his soul, and was a traumatic experience. For him, the cocktail circuit, the social life of Mayfair when he was in London, balanced by a renewed energy in his approach to the Service, gave a the means of escape from his sadness.

From the Service point of view, he became an even more dedicated officer than before, if that were possible. With no distractions other than a young son away at boarding school, and his own inner fight with the continuous pain and disability of his injury, he became absolutely committed to his Service.

But this dedication did not result in the speed of promotion that might have been expected, even at the slow pace of a peacetime Air Force. Trenchard was still king, and he demonstrated an elephantine memory when it came to remembering his displeasure at Reggie's dinner exploit back in '18. Also, of course, having only one leg gave no great impetus to promotion.

Divorce, too, applied a heavy set of brakes to progress up the ladder. Before our enlightened times, marital break-up resulted in a big black mark in the books, and Air Force promotion prospects were no exception. It was not until 1930, when Trenchard had stepped down and the divorce was forgotten that he finally got promoted to Wing Commander.

★   ★   ★

Reggie's Air Staff appointment lasted almost exactly three years. On 8 October 1927 he was back in England, again in an Air Staff appointment, this time with the Chief of the Air Staff's Directorate of Operations at the Air Ministry.

It was during this spell that an old flying friend from the war came back into the picture. Vice Admiral Bell-Davies notes in *Sailor in the Air* that in 1930 '. . . I was appointed liaison officer at the Air Ministry. As there were many old friends from the RNAS there I enjoyed the job. Director of the Operations Directorate to which I was attached was Mills, whom I had known in the RFC, and Reggie Marix was one of his assistants.' The 'small club' feeling was very evident; the RAF was far from the vast organization that it was ultimately to become.

Then in the October of 1929 seven years of staff work took their toll: the flying bug bit again. The official record tells the story: 'Central Flying School, Inland Area, Short Flying Refresher Course from 9.10.29 until 12.10.29.'

A short course indeed. It was thirteen years since his accident had put paid to wartime flying, so he came back to the cockpit of an aircraft far more advanced than those with which he was familiar, and with skills that had lost most of their fine tuning. Moreover, to fly with just one damaged leg represented an additional challenge, one that was to bring fame to Douglas Bader in the second war.

His requalifying instructor was a Flight Lieutenant Day. Day became famous when, as a Wing Commander, he was one of the first RAF prisoners of war captured by the Germans in the 1939-45 war. Not only among the first captured, but also one of the first to escape back to England after having been shot down. He wrote a book – *Wings Day* – about his escape exploit. Later, Nigel met him in the Royal Air Force Club in London, and was intrigued to make this connection with his father's requalification twenty years before.

Once more a pilot, Reggie returned to flying his desk at the Air Ministry for another three years. By now his son Nigel was at Earleywood prep school at Ascot, and of an age to be aware of his father's life. One particular memory was a reminder that the country – in fact, the whole world – was in the middle of the greatest economic depression ever known. The 'Big Crash' on Wall Street happened in October 1929, and its effects continued right up to the beginning of the Second World War.

Reggie had a flat in Dryden Chambers, off Oxford Street, while he was in London. Nigel stayed with him there on occasions. One evening, his father was writing at his desk when there was a ring at the door. It was easier for Nigel to open the door than it was for his father; he found someone asking for 'Reggie.' Reggie asked the caller in. It turned out to be an ex-Lieutenant Commander, pushed out of the Navy after years of service, down on his luck and asking to borrow some money. The conversation ended with Reggie giving him a five pound note to be able to buy some food. Five pounds was a lot of money in those days, and of course the pay of a Squadron Leader was not a King's ransom.

That incident was repeated on many occasions. Once it was an ex-Major in the Royal Flying Corps, who had descended the occupational scale until he was selling vacuum cleaners door to door.

Such was the impact of the economic débâcle of the '30s on the promised 'land fit for heroes to live in.'

On a more personal level, Reggie remained friends with Pixie even after she had remarried in 1934. His ex-wife took as her new husband another sporting hero – Rodney Nickalls, a famous rowing man who had been Captain of Boats at Eton. Rodney's father, Guy Nickalls, was, and probably remains, the only person to have coached both the Oxford and the Cambridge crews. His brother Oliver had also been Eton's Captain of Boats, and later rowed for Oxford. The Nickalls Cup is competed for at Henley to this day.

Nigel remembers the wedding very well. It was held in Paris, and to attend it he had the thrill of his very first flight. A grand chauffeur-driven car collected him from his prep school and delivered him to Hendon Airport. Here he boarded one of the big Imperial Airways passenger biplanes, probably a Hannibal or a Heracles, and flew to France for the ceremony.

The friendliness between the divorced couple deteriorated a little when the decision had to be reached about where the young Nigel would go on after prep school. Reggie wanted Radley; Pixie and her new spouse were all for Eton. They ultimately agreed to disagree, and when the time came the boy was sent to Maiden Erlegh, a private military school.

Reggie broke out of the Air Ministry whenever he could. In 1931 he was an aeronautical test judge on the Schneider Trophy race, a closed-circuit speed event held over the Solent. On that occasion the Supermarine SB6 clocked up 401.5 mph and won the Trophy for Britain outright, the reward for having had three victories in succession against all comers – French, Italians, Americans, and others.

Reggie took Nigel with him to the RAF airship base at Cardington in the early 1930 s when a German passenger airship came in. It was probably the Hindenburg, the counterpart of the ill-fated British R101. When it came in to land, the

captain made a speech to the effect that the last time he had
come to England in a Zeppelin it had been on a bombing
mission. Now, however, he was here as a friend, and a friend he
would remain for evermore!

That visit ended in near-disaster for a number of young
fellows. The RAF category of 'Aircrafthands' described the
most basic airmen whose job it was to move aircraft around.
When it came to airships, their job included holding the craft
down by ropes until it was ready to lift off.

These airmen were in short supply, so a number of local farm
hands were brought in to add their weight. When the command
came to 'let go' two or three of them continued to hang on
grimly, and were hoisted into the air. The sergeant-major (the
old army designations were still in use) yelled 'Let go, you silly
buggers, let go!' This they finally did, fell to the ground with an
awful thud, and broke a number of bones. Luckily no one was
killed, otherwise a Marx Brothers situation could have been
turned into a tragedy.

Meanwhile the political scene in Europe grew more threatening. It was becoming evident that the growth of Fascism and
the rise of the Nazi Party in Germany posed an increasing threat
to European stability and peace. The League of Nations lacked
the teeth to do anything about the renewed descent into chaos;
the western allies – France and Britain particularly – lacked the
political will to oppose Hitler; the United States resolutely
clung to its isolationist doctrines.

But the more perceptive officers in Britain's fighting Services
understood what was going on. Those who had been through
the war to end all wars knew all too clearly that if the menace of
totalitarianism could not be nipped in the bug by the unwilling
democracies, the country would once again by embroiled in a
major conflict. In his position in the Air Staff, Reggie Marix
was among those who knew.

In September 1932 the desk-bound Wing Commander Marix

left the delights of London for his old haunts in the Mediterranean. He was appointed – official wording, again – 'Base Malta, to Command.'

★   ★   ★

Chapter Eleven

Command in Malta

Malta is a flat slab of rock, yellowed as if by age, set as firmly in the tides of European history as it is in the blue Mediterranean Sea. In high summer, it is a hot and arid land, its inhabitants seeking shade in a harsh and nearly treeless environment. Its 120 square miles are home to a third of a million people who trace their roots to millennia of Carthaginian, Arab, Norman, and British influence. Its people in the 1930s lived mostly from the military presence of Great Britain, firmly rooted among the forts and battlements of an earlier age.

One of the most densely populated countries in the world, it was known to the irreverent British serviceman as the land of 'yells, bells, and smells.' The yells came from the dghaiso-men, as they propelled their colourful boats by one oar over the transom, in search of passengers. The incessant clangour of bells came from the churches as they celebrated almost every day the feast of yet another saint in this intensely Catholic land. The smells can be readily imagined, in a tight little island packed with people.

Since World War II Malta suffered an economic crunch following the reduction of the British garrison, became independent, made close friends with some strange bedfellows — Libya, for one — and endured political turmoil when organized labour took on the entrenched power of the Catholic church.

Reggie could have dreamed of none of this when he assumed his command responsibilities. Malta then was as firmly, loyally British as the Rock of Gibraltar, and the changes that were to come were beyond the horizon of any imaginings.

Malta is much more than congestion and noise. It has as much history packed into every stony corner as anywhere else on earth. From the beginnings of time in this most timeless of seas, its development was interwoven with myth and with the stories of the surrounding lands. 1530 was a key date; it was then that the island was given to the Knights of the Order of St John of Jerusalem by Emperor Charles V. With a brief interval when it was captured by Napoleon Bonaparte in 1798, it then remained British from 1800 until becoming independent in 1964.

Only one thing had changed for Reggie in the few short years since his earlier spell of duty in Malta. This time, as a Wing Commander commanding a major air station, he got to know and to be known to the higher echelons of Maltese society.

The Maltese were a pro-British people. Many, if not most, speak at least some English. Just as well: the Maltese tongue is Semitic in origin, and has developed into an impenetrable mixture of Arabic and Sicilian-Italian. The Maltese nobility are a proud and noble breed; they were fond of the British in a snobbish kind of way. But there was a social barrier between them and the British officer cadre, because the British had created an imperial mentality which meant that they always tended to look down on 'the colonials'. Anything as intimate as intermarriage, for example, was taboo. As a result, the 'Malts' tended, understandably enough, to carry a bit of a chip on their shoulders.

Wing Commander Marix, however, was from a different mould than the Maltese were accustomed to. His very unusual and genuine charm, his charismatic flair for making friends, rapidly gained him the respect and affection of a great variety of people, from the highest to the lowest. He showed enormous interest in the island's history; he co-operated with Maltese officialdom whenever an opportunity arose. So high was the esteem in which he was eventually held, he was awarded the signal honour of being made a local Knight of Malta.

When he arrived in 1932, Malta had taken on even more military significance than it had in 1925 at the time of his first appointment to the island. Now, it was vital. As the clouds of war continued to build up, it was evident that the Med would be a crucial area of operations. Britain's fighting services — land, sea and air — were heavily represented on the speck of land which was a combination of aircraft carrier, harbour, and garrison.

Valletta Harbour was the home of the majestic Mediterranean Fleet — battleships, cruisers and destroyers. Submarines, minesweepers, and lesser fleet units were hidden away in other harbours such as Sliema Creek, not so grand but equally useful. Malta dockyard was a major repair and refitting facility, which meant that ships did not have to continually trudge back to home ports to be maintained. The army, including Maltese units, had substantial garrisons. Air, in the form of both Fleet Air Arm and the Royal Air Force, formed a significant part of the military presence.

Life on the tiny island was not all work and no play. There was a light-hearted gaiety about the place, from the lowest sailors' dives in Strait Street (always known for reasons best left to the imagination as 'the Gut') to the highly social life of the upper crust, British and Maltese. There was opera and there were balls, polo and sailing, cocktail parties and swimming parties, the Sliema races and formal dinners.

During these Malta years, the island became very much a part of Nigel's life. He used to go out to stay with his father every summer holiday from school, and sometimes Christmas as well. Vignettes from those days of youthful sunshine and fun illuminate the way Malta was.

In those inter-war years there were no scheduled air services – school children whose parents were based in Malta went out by sea, in ships like the *Largs Bay* and the *Morecambe Bay*, vessels of the Aberdeen and Commonwealth Line. The voyage took about a week, with one brief stop in Gibraltar. The ship would arrive in Valletta Harbour, pass by the lines of battleships and County class cruisers which then were the backbone of the Mediterranean Fleet, and transfer the youngsters into the Governor's launch, or into the pinnaces, pennants flying, of Navy and Air Force officers come to collect their offspring. All this under the eyes of several hundred other passengers – a deeply impressive experience for a schoolboy.

Sometimes Nigel travelled with contemporaries whom he knew quite well. Once he made the trip with the Governor's son, Tony Luke. On another occasion his shipmates were the sons of a Group Captain, John Sowrey, who was subsequently promoted to Air Marshal, as was one of the sons.

Life in Malta for these children of serving officers was a rather grand and privileged one, and contrasted sharply with the more spartan and disciplined life of school. Nigel was only thirteen when his father first took up his command appointment at Hal Far, seventeen when Reggie returned to England. Impressionable years. On the island, he would stay either with his father, or in the home of another married officer where there would be a wife to act as surrogate mother. He was of course too young to be allowed into the RAF officers' mess.

One of Nigel's Malta memories is of his father giving him driving instruction. Reggie had a Morris Cowley which he had modified in the RAF machine shop so that he could drive it with his one leg. Of course, with Nigel driving, the special rig had to be disconnected for normal two-legged driving.

It was during this course of instruction that Nigel gained an insight into his father's personality. He found that Reggie could conform to the conventions of society of the day, while at a deeper level his attitudes were a generation ahead of his time. Long before issues such as 'women's lib' bubbled up into the national consciousness (it was less then twenty years since women had been entitled to vote!) his father's understanding of and respect for women was atypically advanced. But at the same time he could lapse into speech patterns which were locked into contemporary mind-set and prejudice.

Reggie was always extremely attractive to women; he was able to focus on anyone he was talking to as though he was the only person in the world who mattered at that time, and this was doubly true when he was talking with a lady. To the young men of his late Victorian generation, segregated from the opposite sex throughout their early years and right up until they left school – and even after that in the case of service officers, training in all-male establishments – women were at worst the butt of lavatorial jokes, at best a rather embarrassing mystery. In other words, young men were totally ignorant of the psychology of young women. But Reggie cut through all that nonsense – he truly understood women, and this was part of his enormous appeal for them.

But his comprehension of women, his instinctive equal footing with them, was counter to the ethos of the time. Terms like 'the weaker sex' were still common currency. So when Nigel made a particularly expensive-sounding crunch of a gear change, Reggie's comment was 'You're not doing it properly – you're changing gear like a *girl*!' This was a stinging rebuke, and about the biggest insult that you could offer a boy.

Reggie was way ahead of his generation in terms of empathy between the sexes but he had to pay lip-service to the mores of the day. He was a man of deep and very genuine charm, and at the same time perfectly adaptable to the more superficial currents of everyday life.

Adaptability was a keynote. His lifetime spanned an era of immense social change. For example, he saw women's dress evolve from the black and swathing fabrics of the end of the Victorian era to the minimal attire of Brigitte Bardot, and on to the 'swinging sixties.' He took it all in his stride.

Reggie took time from his command position to make sure that his son enjoyed his Malta holidays, even though the rumblings of war were growing louder. Hitler was not the only power-hungry dictator strutting the European stage; Mussolini invaded Abyssinia in 1935, a brutal onslaught against a third world country which the toothless League of Nations was powerless to stop. The British forces in the Mediterranean were on high alert. Malta was potentially under threat from the Italians.

The commanding officer of the destroyer *Wishart* was Lord Louis Mountbatten, with whom Reggie had developed a close friendship. Edwina Mountbatten was also captivated by his charismatic charm, and the three saw a lot of each other. As a result of this friendship, Reggie was able to arrange for Nigel and the two Sowrey boys to spend a day at sea in Mountbatten's ship.

They sailed out from a shoreline bristling with anti-aircraft guns and barbed wire, disincentives to any attack by the forces of Il Duce. So edgy were the admirals that *Wishart*'s exercise torpedo attack on the carrier *Glorious* was cancelled because of the remote possibility that the 'target's' propellors could be hit and damaged. To have a major war vessel out of action for several days at a time of such international tension was a risk they were not prepared to take.

That day at sea was one of rough weather, high waves, much pitching and rolling. Nigel and his friends were on the bridge most of the time with Mountbatten. As they came back into Valletta Harbour, only too pleased to get into its calmer waters, *Wishart*'s propellors became snarled up in some Maltese fishermen's nets. The distant threat of war gave way to the immediate outburst of salty rhetoric, as Lord Louis vented his spleen on the unfortunate locals. For Nigel, it was a baptism of fire in the expert use of impressively bad language.

Afterwards, safely anchored, the boys were invited into the captain's cabin while waiting for a boat to take them ashore. Mountbatten's quarters were lavishly furnished and decorated, like a Mayfair drawing-room – quite different from the more austere accommodation of less illustrious commanding officers.

The son benefited from the father's friendship with Mountbatten by being able to catch an insider's glimpse of the man who was to become one of the towering figures of World War Two. Not only at sea: Mountbatten was a leading polo player, and Reggie often took his son to see the games in which the *Wishart*'s captain was playing.

Nigel benefited also from his father's desire to pass on his flying skills to his son. In the blue skies over summery Malta, Reggie initiated Nigel into the mysteries of piloting an aircraft. He could not allow the boy to do take-offs and landings, because with only one leg his reactions would have been too slow to take over if he made a mistake at a critical juncture. So Reggie would take the Tiger Moth (then the standard RAF basic trainer) up to about three thousand feet, and at that safe height hand over the controls for Nigel to practise turns and other manoeuvres.

Yet another rite of paternal initiation was the mysteries of gambling, which had an additional pay-off in revealing the close friendships which his father had developed with the Maltese. Reggie had inherited a likeness for the gaming table from his own father, and played frequently with the Maltest Marquis of Testaferrato e Braganza in the Malta Casino. In the casino a special room was set aside for members of the Maltese nobility – it was in effect their club.

Reggie was privileged to be invited into this club, where the Marquis, alias 'Bones', who was rolling the dice, said to him, 'I think it would be nice for your son to see inside here.'

The dress rules, however, were strictly enforced, so Reggie replied, 'He's too young to have white tie and tails – he's only got a dinner jacket.'

'Bones' was a small, slightly built man. He quickly came up with the solution. 'My size would be perfect for him. He can borrow mine!'

Which was how Nigel not only got to see this inner sanctum of the Maltese aristocracy, but also came to realise that a very special and rare relationship existed between his father and these people.

Reggie was a man of quiet and unmalicious humour, but he enjoyed occasionally pricking the balloon of pomposity. Over-elaborate church ceremonial was among his targets. One of his favourite stories concerned Lord Louis.

It was Mountbatten's turn to read the lesson in the naval chapel of the garrison in the City of Valletta. Uniform regulations required that he wear full dress for the occasion – frock coat, cocked hat, and a full array of medals. He was handsome, he was impressive, he positively shone with sartorial elegance.

After the service, a very good-looking young mother came up to him and said, 'Lord Louis, you were so wonderful when you read that sermon. My little girl even asked me if you were God!' Mountbatten's straight-faced reply was, 'A very pardonable mistake for the young lady to make, Madam!'

During these Malta years, Reggie demonstrated an inventive flair in two quite different directions – one recreational, the other deadly serious.

Malta was a great place for swimming in those pollution-free days. Clear blue waters lapped up to the rocky shores, the warm summers attracted people into the water, and apart from the risk of treading on the spiny sea urchins there was little or no unpleasant marine life.

Reggie was a keen swimmer, but because of the lack of buoyancy associated with having only one leg he had to wear water wings. He wore goggles for underwater swimming, and then hit upon the idea of taking a spear with him to catch some of the local fish. He designed a properly balanced spear, and had it made in the RAF machine shops at Hal Far. Having to rely on only one leg had made his arms unusually powerful, so he was able to bring up his arm with speed and strength to spear any big fish unlucky enough to come within range.

The idea caught on. Spear fishing became popular among the junior officers in Malta in the '30s . . . probably the very same people who after the Second World War spread the spear fishing technique to places as far afield as Australia and the south of France. Today the sport has developed with highly sophisticated equipment – Scuba gear, underwater lighting, wet suits – and the camera has to a large extent replaced the spear and the harpoon. But it was Reggie Marix who started the ball rolling, and who got people to realise the potential.

The more significant invention was an intercept calculator designed to enable British fighters to come to grips with any air attack on the island very effectively. Based on a triangle of velocities concept, it computed vectors for the defenders to intercept an incoming raid at the greatest possible distance from Malta, thus reducing the numbers of enemy likely to get through. In the days before radar and integrated, computerised fighter defence systems, this innovation marked a major step forward.

Air HQ endorsed the technique. The Air Commodore who dealt with it was encouraged to find that the RAF in Malta had an officer who was inventive enough, and sufficiently aware of the dangers lurking to the north, to come up with such a big contribution to the air defence of the island.

The intercept calculator underscores the fact that the social life of Malta in which Wing Commander Marix played so prominent a part was only the icing on a more serious cake. As Station Commander of the Hal Far base, his responsibilities were akin to those of the captain of a big ship. Operations of the individual squadrons were the duty of the squadron commanders, who reported to him. Reggie, however, was directly accountable for the running of the whole station. With war becoming an increasingly distinct possibility, it fell to him to develop contingency plans to meet any of the forms of attack which might be launched on the island.

As Europe's political climate darkened, these plans became less contingent and more definite. The likelihood of large-scale war increased, even though the governments of Britain and France procrastinated and appeased. The enormous growth of armaments production in the Third Reich could only have one outcome, unless its two major opponents confronted Hitler while there was yet time. This they did not do.

A personal event illustrates the tension of the period. Reggie had agreed with Pixie (with whom he was still on good terms) that Nigel could go and stay in Germany with Paul Winter, a school-mate of his. Relations between the two countries were still cordial enough to allow tourism and exchange of visitors. Both parents were, however, aware of the need for a foreigner travelling in Germany to be on his guard, to say and do nothing to ruffle the feathers of the Nazi regime.

When they were going through the details of the planned visit with Nigel, they took care to explain that the political situation would require caution and a diplomatic approach on his part. But Nigel had been brought up in the anti-German atmosphere of the post war years, and was belligerent and patriotic in the manner of the day. 'You don't expect me to stand up and salute Hitler, do you?'

Reggie sensed trouble. To have his son travel to Germany as a low-profile schoolboy was one thing; to go as a potential teenage rabble-rouser was quite another. 'You know, I don't think that this is such a good idea, after all. If this young man goes to Germany, he's liable to get into all sorts of difficulties.'

So the trip was cancelled. Reggie did not want his son to 'disappear' in Germany of the 1930s as an intransigent Briton.

As a postscript to that visit that never was, the young Paul Winter escaped from Germany immediately before war broke out, and ended up in Syracuse, in the US. He later became a brilliant engineer, and a first class oarsman.

Reggie's outstanding work commanding the Hal Far Base did not go unrecognised. On 1 January 1936 he was promoted to Group Captain, and four months later he transferred to take command of RAF Calafrana, the Malta flying boat base. Here he stayed until November of that year, when he was posted back to the United Kingdom after over four years of command in Malta.

The Maltese word for their own island is 'Melita' – honey, probably from the warm colour of its ancient stone. For Group Captain Marix, his four years of command in the tight little island certainly had elements of honey. His sociable, charismatic personality assured his popularity among his Maltese hosts. The social round was to his liking, insofar as it did not detract from the performance of his duties.

Even with the gathering threat of war, Malta in the thirties was a very *social* place. Rich society matrons in England would send out their daughters to join what was irreverently known as 'the fishing fleet', the bevy of nubile and not-so-nubile young ladies who hoped to trawl up some rich young service officer to be an eventual husband. Hot spot of the social scene was the Sliema Club, where a first rate dance band would play Astaire's 'Top Hat, White Tie, and Tails.' At the opera and the ballet, it was *de rigueur* for the officers to wear full mess dress, in line with the formality of the civilians. A real highlight of the period was when Amy Mollison used Malta as a stopover during her round-the-world flight.

Reggie found time to indulge in another of his recreations in Malta – writing. Plays, skits, and humorous pieces: *Eye of the*

Dingbat and *Money for Jam* were just two of them. He had a sense of the absurd, a Lewis Carroll-like whimsy which was an unusual attribute in the commanding officer of a major air station. One wonders how his subordinates reacted to receiving an important-looking document from 'R L Marix – Very Secret Service Agent', and beginning:

'I have received a cable from the India Office in the Very Highest Grade cypher. It runs as follows:-

TICKETTYBOO. TICKETTYCLICK. OOJAH. RUMBA. BALLYHOO. ZAMBUK. SAHA. BUZZOFF. TUMTUM. WOTROT.

This cypher is of such a high grade that it can only be decyphered by holding everything upside down in front of a looking glass and then multiplying by the number you first thought of . . .'

They must have found it refreshing that the inventor of the intercept calculator and the winner of the DSO over Dusseldorf could have enough of the lighthearted in his nature to produce writing of pure amusement.

One minor irritant of Malta life was the possibility of ailments which the expatriate Briton was unused to. During one of his holiday visits to his father, Nigel Marix contracted 'Malta dog', a dysentery-like sickness carried by the local milk. He was laid low, had to stay on the island, and missed a complete and vital term of school, which scuppered his chances of getting through the entrance exam to the RAF College at Cranwell.

Underlying all the fun, the socialising, the sport, during those years, was the seriousness of purpose with which the Group Captain took his responsibilities. Having fought an extraordinary war, in the air and on land, less than twenty years earlier, he was fully sensitive to the implications of getting into another one. When the laughing stopped, as it would do not much more than three years after he relinquished command of the Calafrana base to return home, one-legged Reggie Marix would be as purposeful and dedicated as any officer in the inter-war Royal Air Force.

Chapter Twelve

Coastal Command

When Group Captain Marix returned to Britain at the end of 1936 he was able to fit in a few weeks' leave before taking up his next appointment on 1 February 1937 – Senior Air Staff Officer at the Lee-on-Solent Headquarters of 16 Group, Coastal Command. He was promoted to the rank of Acting Air Commodore on 23 August 1939, and on the outbreak of war on 3 September 1939 he was promoted to Acting Air Vice Marshal, and took command of the Group.

A groundswell of change in the country's mood and preoccupations had taken place in the four years that Reggie had been away in Malta. Among those whom Keynes called 'the Ins' – the politically aware minority – Hitler's rise to power in the earlier part of the decade had sharpened the cutting edge of the argument between Fascism and Communism. Fascism was best exemplified by the parades of Oswald Mosley's Blackshirts, in the East End of London, and by the activities of the British Union of Fascists in general. Communism's front runners in Britain included people like Gollancz, Laski, and Strachey, of the Left Book Club.

But for the hoi polloi the 1930s were, at least until the end of the decade, years of slow recovery from the great depression, years of cricket and football, of the maturing of radio and the advent of television, of the talkies and coloured movies. *Panem et circenses*, in short; years of peace. The great majority of the British public were politically asleep until 1938, when a sudden awareness of what was going on broke upon them.

The 'Ins' knew that major international trouble was brewing. The man (and woman) in the street were focused on quite another scene in 1936. The love affair between King Edward VIII and the twice-divorced Mrs Wallis Simpson unfolded rapidly to the astonished plebeian gaze. The British media had kept the lid on the cauldron which was bubbling in Court and government circles, even though it was in the gossip columns of Europe and the United States.

The royal crisis was unveiled for the first time in the daily newspapers on 2 December. On 11 December, just nine days later, the King abdicated in favour of his brother Albert, Duke of York, who took the title of George VI. The Abdication (the capital 'A' became almost mandatory) fizzed like a firework through the national consciousness, and was seen at the time as being of the gravest constitutional and national importance. So ephemeral is the public attention-span, however, that the affair rapidly deteriorated into a non-event. The new King dedicated himself with a large measure of success to his unexpected role. The Duke of Windsor and his Duchess were relegated to the sidelines of history, and became somewhat forlorn members of the international set of displaced European royals.

Meanwhile, the Spanish Civil War's outbreak in the summer of 1936 added fuel to the glowing fire of European unrest, with support for both opposing sides being provided by individuals from an officially non-partisan Britain. The Fascist threat came into clearer focus; the earlier Abyssinian crisis and Germany's reoccupation of the Rhineland had already, as A. J. P. Taylor writes in *English History 1914-1945*, 'shattered the easy security of the postwar years.' Hitler's path to war seemed – at least to the 'Ins' – to be beyond question. The man in the street was at most a little uneasy about the tangled machinations in distant Europe.

How did all this affect Reggie Marix? March 1935 was a watershed month in the shaping of the air war that was to come. It was then that Hitler told Sir John Simon that Germany had reached parity in the air with Great Britain. 'The British service chiefs,' writes Taylor, 'took German figures at their face value, or rather regarded them as less than the reality. The truth was exactly the reverse: Germany never had the arms she claimed to have . . . The British air chiefs pushed up their (rearmament) estimates of German arms.'

So Reggie came back into a situation in which the expansion of the Royal Air Force was going on at a colossal speed, in absolute terms as well as in terms of comparison with the perceived threat from Nazi Germany. Taylor again:

'The British air staff . . . further overrated the number of aeroplanes which Germany possessed and, still more, of those which she would soon possess. In 1938, for example, they estimated the German frontline strength at twice the British, and future German production at twice the British also. Actual German superiority then was only 60 per cent in frontline strength; reserves were less than the British; trained pilots equal. British production of aeroplanes had almost reached the German level and surpassed it in the course of 1939 . . . In 1935 the RAF received only half the money spent on the army and less than a quarter of that spent on the navy. By 1939 it was receiving more money than either of the other forces.'

A heady atmosphere. The RAF – particularly the heavy bomber – was positioned as the chief counter to the Nazi challenge. Trenchard's influence continued to be exerted on the direction that air strategy was taking. He had been Chief of the Air Staff from 1919 to 1929, when the policy that heavy bombing could win a war all by itself became an accepted tenet of the RAF's philosophy. That tenet was very much to the forefront during the late 1930 s, to the detriment of air defence of the British Isles.

In Reggie's time as Senior Air Staff Officer in his Coastal Command Group, the threat was assessed by the top air chiefs as being primarily that of massive air raids on Britain. In the event, and with the benefit of hindsight, we know that the potential of Germany to inflict damage on the civilian population was grotesquely over-estimated. Taylor:

> 'British experts . . . exaggerated the effect of bombing – their own, of course, as much as the Germans. In 1937 they expected an attack continuing for sixty days, with casualties of 600,000 dead and 1,200,000 injured. The ministry of health, advised by these experts, calculated in 1939 that from one million to three million hospital beds would be needed immediately after the outbreak of war. Actual civilian casualties from air attack in Great Britain during nearly six years of war were 295,000, of whom 60,000 were killed.'

Massive retaliation was seen as being the only defence, meaning that Bomber Command would be the priority arm for development in those years. 'Bomber' Harris and the strategy of destroying the German economy and morale by means of aerial bombardment were the natural result of this Trenchardian thinking, which entailed the loss of more than 50,000 aircrew for the reduction of perhaps one per cent of Nazi war production. Taylor argues that 'the chiefs of the RAF always put independent bombing first and grudged the tiresome distractions of fighter and coastal command.'

Today those massive night raids over Germany are almost inconceivable. As many as a thousand or even two thousand heavy bombers at a time, with an attrition rate which meant that after a twenty sortie tour of operations an airman's number was statistically up. Night after night these raids went on at the height of the war. The gallantry and self-sacrifice of the aircrews can now only be caught at second hand, in such brilliantly descriptive books as Len Deighton's *Bomber*. At the time, the losses were as severe as one of the major battles of the first World War. It was only when the nation had the time to lick its wounds after the war that the airmen's dedication was fully understood.

And yet, despite the two decades of concentration on massive saturation bombing of the enemy, it was 'the few' of Fighter Command under Dowding who in 1940 finally crushed any dream of German invasion of the British Isles. Dowding went into the Battle of Britain with fifty-five squadrons, consisting mainly of aircraft which were in most respects at least the equivalent of their German opponents. He also held the ace in the pack – radar, enabling precise control of the fighter squadrons to home accurately on the attackers. He was, however, very short of reserves of trained pilots, and this would have been his Achilles heel had it not been for the stamina and determination of the 'few' that he had.

It was Coastal Command whose surveillance of home waters, and above all the relentless hounding of the U-boat, played a key role in securing the continued survival of the island nation. Under the inspired leadership of its Commander-in-Chief, Air Marshal 'Ginger' Bowhill, it became the scourge of German submarines. Bowhill had been a sailor long before going into aviation, and had even trained under sail as a young officer. His intimate knowledge of the sea undoubtedly contributed a great deal to the ultimate mastery of the U-boat.

'Coastal' only achieved independent status in 1936, so Reggie Marix was taking up his responsibilities in a new organization. Susanne Everett, in *Wars of the Twentieth Century*:

'In 1937 it was agreed that 291 aircraft should be allotted
to it for convoy escort and reconnaissance duties over
the North Sea. Another 48 were to be stationed at
convoy assembly points abroad. By 1939 less than two-
thirds of this modest total were available, and they were
slow and obsolescent Ansons.'

A 'tiresome distraction' indeed. But during Reggie's time with
the Command, it flowered into an arm of air strategy which
played a vital, perhaps even decisive, role in eroding the ability
of the *unterseebooten* to savage Britain's sea links.

Two sets of figures illustrate the point. In 1942, one of the
worst periods for merchant shipping losses, 1,164 Allied ships
were lost, of which 1,160 were sunk by U-boats – more than
three a day. But of the 1,162 submarines that the Germans
commissioned during the war, 785 were sunk – 245 of them by
shore-based aircraft.

All that was then in the future. Group Captain Marix had
nearly three years to serve as Senior Air Staff Officer of the
Group, from the King's abdication through Munich and the
1938 Czechoslovakian crisis, until the culmination of events
when Germany invaded Poland on 1 September 1939, to be
followed by Britain's declaration of war two days later.

The previous Air Officer Commanding had suffered an injury. As a result, Reggie took temporary command of 16
Group, with acting Air rank, with effect from the very day war
was declared.

★ ★ ★

The Group was now based at Chatham. When Reggie took
over, he found himself with the established responsibilities of
Coastal Command – protection of shipping, anti-submarine and
long-range maritime patrols, and air sea rescue. The aircraft he

controlled were a pretty ancient lot – Avro Ansons, old flying boats, a collection of biplanes. Many of them were museum pieces, comparable to the Fleet Air Arm's obsolescent Skuas, Sea Gladiators, Swordfish, and Rocs. But they soon got a handful of the brand new and outstandingly successful Beaufighters, and two squadrons were equipped with Sunderland flying boats.

Coastal Command, it must be remembered, along with Fighter Command, had been a 'tiresome distraction', and could not expect to be at the front of the queue when it came to receiving new and more effective aircraft. But in spite of outdated equipment, U-boats soon had to modify their ideas about charging batteries on the surface when they found themselves under attack by Sunderlands using bombs and pre-set depth charges.

After just four months, on 8 January 1940, a substantive Air Vice Marshal was appointed to take over command of the Group from Reggie's temporary guardianship. The job he had been doing was more than usually appreciated; he received a personal letter from the Officers' Appointments department of the Air Ministry which broke the news to him gently. It was dated 16 December 1939, and read:

> 'Dear Marix,
>
> You will shortly be called upon to give up the command of No. 16 Group in order to make way for an officer of the correct substantive rank, and I should not like this to happen without my putting on record my very high appreciation of the excellent work you have done in command of the Group since your former A.O.C. was injured, and particularly since the outbreak of war.
>
> I am sure you will appreciate that the grant of acting rank to an officer automatically involves him in the

liability to disappointment when it has to be surrendered, and I hope that your very natural regret at having to leave your Group at a time when it is doing such splendid work will be tempered by the satisfaction of knowing that you have done well and that equally important work awaits you at Coastal Command Headquarters.'

Acting Air Commodore Marix took up his new appointment as Deputy Senior Air Staff Officer at Coastal Command HQ as soon as he left Chatham. He remained there for a year, with a brief return to Chatham to command 16 Group in February and March of 1940. Working in the 'nerve centre' of Coastal he was at the very heart of development of new tactics and the introduction of new aircraft as the need for more effective anti-submarine defence grew.

At the end of his spell at HQ, Reggie did a brief stint of a month or two in command of 20 Group, a training centre. Few details of this period of his career are on the record, but he liked to recount one anecdote from his fund of humorous stories.

Dame Trefusis Forbes was then Commandant of the WAAF – the Women's Auxiliary Air Force. She decided that it would be a good idea to visit her young ladies in the training group. She asked her personal assistant to arrange the visit, and a signal was accordingly sent to 20 Group which was received as: 'COMMANDANT PLANS TO VISIT THE WAAFS SUNDAY 14TH. SHE LIKES PIMMS'.

The Acting Air Vice Marshal dutifully made sure that the officers' mess would be made ready with jugs of Pimms Number One, and then went to meet Dame Trefusis at the main gate. He accompanied her around the station along with his senior WAAF officer, planning the visit to last for an hour before the mess bar opened.

Right on the dot of noon, Dame Trefusis, Reggie, and the senior WAAF officer went into the mess. Reggie looked at the visitor with his hypnotic blue eyes. 'I've got just what you want,' he said. 'Try this.'

Dame Trefusis took a sip of the glass of Pimms which he handed her. 'Wonderful!' she said. 'Just like lemonade.'

Reggie laughed. 'Yes, *just* like lemonade.'

The uniformed lady thereupon swallowed the entire contents of the glass, closely followed by a second.

She blinked, and looked slightly disorientated. 'You know,' she said, 'I am feeling just a little bit giddy.'

'Well,' said Reggie, 'you have had two glasses, you know, and it's just what you asked for – Pimm's.'

'Pimm's?' exclaimed the Dame. '*Pimm's*? I asked for *hymns*! I was wondering when we were going to arrive at the church!'

After this brief interlude in training, on 24 March 1941 he was back in the thick of things, again as Acting Air Vice Marshal, this time commanding 18 Group Coastal Command, with his headquarters in Pitreavie Castle, on the east coast of Scotland. As AOC, he had the benefit of an official residence, a lovely house with sweeping views over the Firth of Forth. The officers' mess was at Dunfermline, on the north side of the Forth.

★   ★   ★

1941 was perhaps the darkest year of the war for Britain. The nation stood alone against a German-dominated Europe. Pearl Harbour was not attacked by the Japanese until the end of the year, finally bringing America into the war. It was not until June that Hitler launched Operation Barbarossa and made the classic, Napoleonic mistake of invading the Soviet Union.

As far as Coastal Command was concerned, it was a year of rapidly intensifying war against the U-boats. The Atlantic was

Britain's lifeline, and it was there that Doeniz concentrated his greatest efforts. Group tactics were introduced, in which individual submarines were vectored in along a convoy's track to form 'wolf packs' with catastrophic results for the merchantmen. Long-range reconnaissance aircraft, the famous Focke-Wulf Kondors, were able to spot convoys and radio sighting reports to U-boat HQ.

In spite of the 'destroyers for bases' deal of late 1940, when fifty old American 'four-stackers' were handed over to Britain, the Royal Navy remained critically short of suitable anti-submarine vessels. Such escorts as there were suffered from limited range frigates based in Halifax, Nova Scotia, for example, and employed on convoy escort duty, would have to return to refuel long before meeting up with other ships sent out from a British port to meet the incoming merchantmen. This mid-ocean gap was fully exploited by the German submarines.

There were few and inadequate carriers at that stage in the war to provide seaborne air escort for the vulnerable convoys, and it soon became evident that long range land-based anti-submarine aircraft were becoming the most effective means of stemming the losses. This aspect of the war at sea developed into the prime focus of Coastal Command.

Reggie's 18 Group was fully committed to the anti-submarine war, but did not lose sight of other operations which were Coastal's responsibility. More and newer aircraft were by then becoming available, enabling the Command to extend its remit beyond the defensive and protective roles which had been its normal bailiwick. In fact, as AOC, Reggie himself was very personally involved in one of the more dramatic operations. This was an offensive action which made headlines in the press at a time when every possible boost to public morale was needed.

On 29 October the Hudsons of 18 Group's 220 Squadron flew from Scotland to Aalesund, in Norway, to attack German

shipping and installations. Reggie decided to go along to observe the action, and took a place in the lead aircraft. Of course,
it was not standard operating procedure to have the Air Officer
Commanding go along for the ride. It was even less usual for the
AOC in question to have only one leg – twenty-five years had
elapsed since his crash in France during the First World War.

The Flight Sergeant who helped Marix into the Hudson
made ready to buckle up his parachute. Reggie would have
none of it; he pointed out to the Sergeant that if the aircraft was
shot down he would be unable to get out anyway with only one
leg to manoeuvre with. 'Thank you, but I'm much sooner be
comfortable!' Reggie's disdain for the dangers of a raid over
enemy-held territory was to have repercussions later.

The attack itself is best related by Andrew Hendrie, in his
book *Seek and Strike*:

> 'The Squadron's Hudsons were all airborne from Wick
> by 4.10 p.m. and within six minutes of each other. They
> were led by Wing Commander Wright, who had as pas-
> senger in aircraft G, Air Vice Marshal Marix, the AOC.
>
> 'On such trips one hoped for enough cloud cover in
> which to escape but with visibility sufficiently good for
> the enemy to be spotted. Ships of both sides seemed only
> too pleased to fire at any Hudson foolish or unlucky
> enough to get too close; and on the Norwegian side,
> there were experienced German fighter pilots no less
> hostile.
>
> 'The Hudsons would have crossed the North Sea to
> that part of Norway in about two hours. Wing Com-
> mander Wright, who had been the first to take off,
> sighted a merchant vessel in Aalesund which he attacked
> despite intensive light flak. He saw only thick smoke as a
> result of his bombing, but other crews later stated that
> the ship caught fire and was sinking.

'Hudson M, captained by Sergeant Houghton, saw another vessel in the entrance to Nord fjord. He attacked. There was a violent explosion and portions of the deck and superstructure of the ship were blasted into the air. This was followed by clouds of steam and smoke. Two merchant vessels close alongside the Aalesund shore were bombed by Flying Office Holland, although he saw no results. One of his crew was wounded in the leg during the intense flak which was suffered.

'Pilot Officer Tate, in D, attacked the harbour installations to the west of Aalesund and confirmed damage to three ships which he saw burning in the harbour.

'No 220 Squadron's strike must have been as intensive as the flak they were prepared to fly through; Flying Officer Birchall's bombing of an escort vessel silenced its guns, Flying Officer Tarrant in K scored a hit on a merchant vessel, gunned defences and drove a lorry off the road, dropped incendiaries on a fish oil factory and started a fire.

'The squadron record does not specify the bomb loads of the nine Hudsons but it would appear likely that four 250 lb bombs could have been carried by some of the aircraft. Hits were claimed on another ship in the harbour by Squadron Leader Barron who attacked from 1500 feet and who saw the vessel sink. Sergeant 'Henry' Hall bombed two merchant vessels, one of which was already on fire. It was seen to sink.

'All nine Hudsons made some attack on the enemy, even Sergeant Heppell in E. He suffered a blown fuse when over the target. They all returned to Wick, with only A being damaged by flak, and one of the gunners in U suffering a leg wound. The score for the enemy was much more serious; a German merchant vessel of 3,101 tons was sunk – *Barcelona* – and two Norwegian ships under the control of the enemy were damaged. They were each of over 1,000 tons – the *Swanefjell* and *Vesla*. It seems likely that the enemy lost much more than is listed by Coastal Command.

'The 220 Squadron scribe has 'spread' himself by putting in the record 'AALESUND STRIKE'! It was a remarkable achievement by any standard, but particularly bearing in mind the bomb load of the Hudson (typically 1,000 lbs), its defensive armament, and maximum speed. To put it in perspective, this raid should be contrasted with the No 2 Group Bomber Command raids on docks and shipping, and the later Beaufighter/Torbeau strikes which enjoyed a strong fighter escort of Spitfires or Mustangs.

'It was probably this raid which was depicted by an official war artist on a National Savings poster circa 1941–42.'

The press made the most of this morale-booster. 'RAF HAMMER BLOWS ON SHIPPING' ran one headline. 'THE MOST DEVASTATING ATTACK BY SINGLE SQUADRON.' '4 VESSELS SUNK, 3 CRIPPLED, AND HARBOUR WRECKED.' For Britain to see that it was carrying the war to the enemy was a light in the gloom of 1941.

After this daring attack, Reggie threw a bit party at one of the big Edinburgh hotels for all the aircrew involved. It was a major event, with champagne flowing – much more in the style of the RFC and RNAS days of the First World War than of the melancholia of 1941. For an Air Vice Marshal to entertain his men in this way was perhaps unique. But then Reggie in his own style was a unique officer.

There were repercussions, however – not relating to the party, but simply because as an officer of Air rank he had, in the eyes of the top brass, needlessly exposed himself to the risks inherent in a sortie of this type. He was discreetly hauled over the coals, and orders were subsequently issued that officers at that senior level were not to fly operationally without the specific approval of their Commander in Chief or of the Chief of the Air Staff. Air officers with the vast experience of men like Reggie Marix were in very short supply; exploits which risked their lives unnecessarily were viewed in a poor light.

Repercussions or not, the episode illustrated Reggie's aggressive spirit. With the flak coming up thick and fast at his lead Hudson over Aalesund, his thoughts must surely have gone back twenty-seven years to October 1914, to Dusseldorf, his tiny Sopwith Tabloid, and the blazing Zeppelin. The technology had changed: Reggie's character hadn't.

Chapter Thirteen

From Coastal to Canada

By the time of the Aalesund exploit, Reggie was coming to the end of his several years at senior levels in Coastal Command. During that time he had played a major role in transforming Coastal from a relative backwater into a force at the cutting edge of Britain's continued struggle, a struggle not yet for victory, but for survival. Victory was still a long way in the future. The Battle of Britain had ensured that Hitler's Operation Sealion, the planned invasion of Britain, would never take place. But there was a lot of fighting – land, sea and air – to be done before the ultimate victory would be more than a distant goal.

Vice Admiral Sir Arthur ('Baldy') Hezlet, in *Aircraft and Sea Power*, paints a vivid picture of the rapid escalation of Coastal's role in the defence of the island. 'After the Norwegian campaign', he writes, 'and during the summer of 1940, the Germans turned increasingly to an attack on British commerce and on 17th August Hitler ordered a total blockade of the British Isles. To enforce this blockade, U-boats, aircraft, surface raiders and mines were all used . . .'

These attempts to isolate the country provided the impetus for Coastal Command's growth and increasing breadth of roles. 'Coastal Command', Hezlet continues, 'had increased in strength since the beginning of the war from 265 aircraft at the

outset to 490 by 1st July 1940. The main increase is accounted
for by the addition of 93 long-range fighters and some 50
torpedo-bombers. There were, however, 64 more general reconnaissance machines and a greater proportion of this type
were now medium-ranged Hudsons and Sunderlands instead of
the very short-ranged Ansons . . .

'Coastal Command had grown to a total of 564 aircraft by the
beginning of 1941 with a slightly higher proportion of aircraft
of medium range than before . . . by the end of the year Coastal
Command had expanded to 633 aircraft and the short-range
Anson and London types had practically all been replaced.'

Hezlet points out that more than two millions tons of Allied
shipping were sunk by U-boats in 1941. In March of that year,
Churchill gave an extremely high priority to the Battle of the
Atlantic, and to meet the threat the re-equipping of Coastal
went on apace throughout the time that Reggie was commanding 18 Group. Short-range London flying boats were replaced
by Catalinas, with more than double the operating radius. Some
Groups received Whitleys, Wellingtons, and later in the year
B24 Liberators – all with the aim of extending effective air
cover for convoys and forcing the German submarines into
deep field.

Reggie's years in Coastal were exciting ones, culminating in
greatly enhanced capability and power for the young Command. They were good ones, too, for Reggie. He had been
made a Companion of the Order of the Bath in July 1940, a
year after having been promoted to Air rank. His unusual
ability to get on with all sorts and conditions of men had suited
him ideally to weld together a Group which, during this phase
of unprecedented growth, came to consist of a much broader
variety of men and women than the tight little pre-war club of
the RAF.

Hitherto, the officer corps had consisted of a close-knit fraternity of aviators feeling a spiritual kinship with the cavalry

and with naval officers from whom the RFC and the RNAS had originally been formed, and whose devil-may-care, élitist philosophy they inherited. The RAF of the 'thirties worked hard and played hard − it took professionalism to the outer limits in terms of flying and fighting ability, but when off duty its officers were allowed remarkable scope for their individualism.

Now it had swollen into a microcosm of the country at large − in fact, of the whole British Commonwealth. Promotions from the ranks were made at a dizzying pace; Australians, New Zealanders, Canadians, men from all over the Empire joined together with what had been an almost exclusively British force. To engender high morale, sense of purpose, and group cohesiveness needed a leader with a special brand of leadership. Reggie was that man.

War wrought in his character a subtle change of emphasis. He was still the same confidence-inspiring figure, but gone where the raucous mess evenings in Malta with the Station Commander playing the piano for the obvious enjoyment and delight of his singing junior officers, the light-hearted fun and games of the pre-war RAF. Reggie enjoyed the social side of service life, but the self-imposed discipline with which he met the challenge of war created in him a spirit of dedication and gave an almost monastic pattern to his days.

'Early to bed, early to rise.' No more parties. The responsibilities of a Coastal Command AOC needed a 'hands on' attitude. He was in the Operations Room from early in the morning until late in the evening, on deck and in control in the same way as the captain of a ship in action.

His streak of inventiveness still found time to express itself. In 1940, he had made a proposal to the Ministry of Aircraft Production for a special bomb fuse. He must have been disappointed to have been beaten to the post; in January 1941 the Ministry's Director of Contracts acknowledged his idea:

MINISTRY OF AIRCRAFT PRODUCTION
HARROGATE
YORKS
30th January 1941

Invention relating to Anti-disturbance Fuse

Sir,

With reference to your letter of the 11th October, 1940, in the above matter, I am directed to state that the particulars of your proposal have been examined by the technical department. It is reported that the proposal is ingenious and would work provided that the suspension of the pear and ball switch can be made to withstand the high deceleration experienced by a bomb on impact and can at the same time remain sensitive. It is stated, however, that the apparatus as designed would be expensive to produce and the electrical connections fragile and that a device giving similar results which is more robust, more easily manufactured and likely to be reliable, is now in the course of production.

In the circumstances it is not proposed to take any further action in connection with your invention and an application for patent will not be filed at public expense. You may, however, obtain patent protection for the device at your own expense if you wish to do so, but it is considered that the invention should be kept secret, so if you wish to take this course will you please be good enough to inform this Department before the application is filled in order that the necessary precautions may be taken.

The Department wishes me to thank you for submitting this suggestion for consideration and for the trouble you have taken in preparing the design . . .

One is tempted to chuckle at the idea of the Ministry's giving Reggie the idea of patenting his fuse privately, albeit under conditions of secrecy. After all, how many customers for such a device would he have been likely to find in a war-torn Europe other than the self-same Ministry of Aircraft Production?

A disappointment, certainly. But the episode shows that the innovative flame that created the intercept calculator in Malta was burning even brighter with the incentive of war.

★　★　★

In February 1942 Reggie's long association with Coastal Command came to an end. He was appointed to HQ 18 Group 'supernumerary pending posting overseas.' On 8 March a new and entirely different chapter of his service life opened: he became the Senior Air Staff Officer for Royal Air Force Ferry Command in Canada.

The *raison d'être* of Ferry Command is best expressed in a letter written by Winston Churchill to Franklin D. Roosevelt on 8 December 1940. The Prime Minister's letter was written at a time when the immediate invasion threat to Britain had receded, leaving the prospect of a long, hard, grinding war. It was also at a time when the policy of 'cash and carry' in Britain's purchases of war supplies from the United States was running out of steam – the country's cash reserves were nearing exhaustion.

The communication from the PM was designed to appeal to the President's sense of common purpose between the US and the United Kingdom, and to seek for increasing flows of material so that Britain, standing alone in the fight against Nazism, could pursue that common purpose successfully. In this it was successful: it initiated Roosevelt's presentation to Congress of the famous Lend-Lease Bill, and ensured that Britain would not be knocked out of the war for lack of the arms to carry it through.

One paragraph from Churchill's letter gives a startlingly clear exposition of the size and scope of the numbers of military aircraft requested from the American President. No further commentary is needed to explain the existence of a Ferry Command to bring them across the Atlantic and into the theatre of European operations:

'. . . we look to the industrial energy of the Republic for a reinforcement of our domestic capacity to manufacture combat aircraft. Without that reinforcement reaching us in substantial measure we shall not achieve the massive preponderance in the air on which we must rely to loosen and disintegrate the German grip on Europe. We are at present engaged on a programme designed to increase our strength to seven thousand first-line aircraft by the spring of 1942. But it is abundantly clear that this programme will not suffice to give us the weight of superiority which will force open the doors of victory. In order to achieve such superiority it is plain that we shall need the greatest production of aircraft which the United States of America is capable of sending us. It is our anxious hope that in the teeth of continuous bombardment we shall realise the greater part of the production which we have planned in this country. But not even with the addition to our squadrons of all the aircraft which, under present arrangements, we may derive from planned output in the United States can we hope to achieve the necessary ascendancy. May I invite you then, Mr President, to give earnest consideration to an immediate order on joint account for a further two thousand combat aircraft a month? Of these aircraft, I would submit, the highest possible proportion should be heavy bombers, the weapon on which, above all others, we depend to shatter the foundations of German power. I am aware of the formidable task that this would impose upon the industrial organisation of the United States.

Yet, in our heavy need, we call with confidence to the most re-sourceful and ingenious technicians in the world. We ask for an unexampled effort, believing that it can be made.'

Churchillian rhetoric and Roosevelt's appreciation of the threat Nazi aggression posed to the whole world won the day. It became the task of Ferry Command to organize a one-way stream of medium and large aircraft from the factories of America to the European theatre of operations.

Essentially, the Command operated from Dorval, near Montreal, with the brief of bringing together these huge numbers of aircraft, flying them across the Atlantic, and getting the crews back again for the next trip. Reggie Marix joined an organization which been operating for nearly eighteen months – an operation which many experts had pronounced 'impossible'!

No one tells the tale from an aircraft captain's perspective better than Don Teel, who was involved with the task throughout the war. He made these points in a speech to a combined meeting of 'World War 1 Pilots' and 'War Birds of the RAF' at the Breakers Hotel in Palm Beach on November 11 1978:

On 11 November 1940, at 0850 GMT, the first American-built bomber to be flown across the Atlantic for delivery to the Royal Air Force landed at Aldergrove aerodrome. It was a Lockheed Hudson, flown by Group Captain (later Air Vice Marshal) D.C.T. Bennett, leader of a formation of seven which had departed from Gander, Newfoundland, the evening before. The other six aircraft all landed safely within the hour.

The North Atlantic had never before been flown in either direction in winter. Most experts said that at the then stage of aviation development, it could not be done!

This contribution to the conquest of the Atlantic by land planes cannot be rated too highly. It was the opening of the bottleneck of getting American-built bombers to Britain, and is really the grandfather of our present international airlines. It spelled the beginning of the end for the large seaplane.

Major decisions hung on the result of that first flight. Had it not been successful, the whole ferrying concept could well have been abandoned, with untold impact on the conduct of the war in Europe.

The criterion for 'success' was that fifty per cent of the aircraft should get through safely. Better than that half-way mark, and the project would go ahead; worse, and it would have been given up. It is a measure of the extreme need of the RAF for those aircraft at that stage of the war that the project organizers would have accepted an attrition rate of fifty per cent. And it is a sobering thought that those early crews faced, in the view of the experts, no better than an even chance of making it across the wintry north Atlantic.

A second formation of seven Hudsons arrived safely in Britain on 30 November, a third on 18 December. Captain Bennett meanwhile had returned to Montreal by ship, and led the fourth group across at the end of December. From this flight of seven, only four reached Britain. One crashed on takeoff, but with no injury to the crew; another was unable to take off from Gander because of a wreck on the runway; and a third had to return because of engine trouble.

From 11 November to the end of the year, the new-born ferry group had delivered twenty-five out of a possible twenty-eight badly needed bombers to England with no injury to any crew member, and the loss of only one aircraft. They had done what the experts had said was impossible!

And that, of course, was only the beginning. Ferry Command delivered a grand total of more than ten thousand aircraft before the war ended.

Don Teel went on to comment on the fact that initially the Command was an all-civilian organization, operating under orders from the Ministry of Aircraft Production and administered by Canadian Pacific Railways. Not until August 1941 did it come under the control of the Air Ministry and take on the letters 'RAF' before the designation 'Ferry Command'. So at the time that Reggie was assigned to Canada, it had only been a Royal Air Force responsibility for a few months.

Air Marshal Sir Frederick ('Ginger') Bowhill, who had played so significant a role as Commander-in-Chief of Coastal Command, took over the whole operation. It became a strange and unprecedented mixture of service and civilian aircrew and ground staff, symbolised by Don Teel's own crew: himself, an American civilian, captain; a Lieutenant RNZAF as co-pilot; a Squadron Leader, RAAF as navigator; an RAF sergeant as engineer; a Canadian civilian radio operator; and an RAF airman as purser. Don had no trouble at all in working with this international mix of civilians and servicemen – they were, in this own words, 'a wonderful crew'.

The main task of Ferry Command, then, as Reggie took over his new responsibilities, was to deliver aircraft (and sometimes other war supplies) to British and Allied air forces throughout the war. This it did supremely well, with an exemplary safety record.

From early in 1942, it operated another, highly specialised, detachment. Originally known as Communications Flight, it was later renamed 231 Squadron, and began as a means of getting critically needed equipment across the South Atlantic and central Africa into Cairo to help repulse Rommel's push to Egypt. Returning aircraft were used to bring back returning ferry crews.

231 Squadron eventually became a kind of wartime VIP airline, carrying passengers like Winston Churchill and Lord Mountbatten to destinations as dispersed as Prestwick, Karachi, Accra, Sydney, Moscow, Tehran, and Chungking.

★   ★   ★

Such was the ad hoc, unorthodox, but highly effective organisation that Reggie Marix joined as Senior Air Staff Officer in March 1942. It would be a different war for him, a war far removed from the close-up action which he had experienced in both world conflicts. But he knew very well that the success of Ferry Command was vital to the survival and rebuilding of Britain and its armed forces.

Chapter Fourteen

Ferry Command

1942 was a decisive year in the Allies' struggle against Germany in the European theatre. America was now in the war. The Japanese attack on Pearl Harbor on 7 December 1941 had ensured that the mighty industrial economy of the United Sates would be dedicated to the overthrow of the Axis powers. Eventual victory was virtually a foregone conclusion.

Before that victory, however, years of grinding struggle were to take place. The first few months of 1942 saw massive defeats. Singapore fell to the Japanese in February. In the same month seventy-one ships totalling 384,000 tons were sunk in the Atlantic, the heaviest losses in the war to that point. Almost all were in the American zone, where the US Navy had been unprepared for such an onslaught.

Winston Churchill wrote in *The Hinge of Fate*: 'To us in the British Isles it seemed that everything was growing worse, although on reflection we knew that the war was won.' On reflection, yes; but a senior RAF officer had scant time for meditation at that point in the conflict.

Coastal Command's war in the waters of the North Atlantic and the North Sea was dour and demanding. As AOC 18 Group, Reggie had known that his aircrews were continually pitted against a determined and wily enemy. They also had to contend with a harsh climatic environment: flying con-

117

ditions, especially in winter, were seldom friendly to the aviator.

Back at base, it was not easy for the crews to relax after the
tensions and dangers of long and stressful anti-submarine
patrols. Airfields were often situated in remote and climatically
inhospitable parts of Scotland – Wick, Arbroath, Lossiemouth –
where entertainment and diversion outside the mess were at a
premium. Food for service men and women was adequate but
unexciting, petrol for private use (even if one had access to a
vehicle) was virtually non-existent. Night fell early in the winter months. Life was hard.

When Reggie took up his new appointment in March 1942
he entered a world sharply in contrast with the grey, grim slog
of Coastal Command's wearing war of attrition. North America
was still the land of milk and honey. The demands of total war
in 1942 had a relatively minor impact on the giant economies of
the US and Canada, or on the way of life of their citizens.
Reggie's diary for that year reflects the change of mood.

As he set off, the first leg of his journey merely exchanges
one hard set of weather conditions for another.

Tuesday March 3	Left London for Prestwick by night train.
Wednesday March 4	Expect to leave for Canada tonight.
Thursday March 5	Called at 0100 but departure postponed on met reports.
Sunday March 8	Left Prestwick in Liberator at 0645 for arrival in Gander in Newfoundland at 1400 local time. Arrived 1½ hours ahead of time . . . bad met. report from Montreal prevented continuance. Shown round Camp by Mackay, the Traffic officer. Snow and slush made roads in very bad condition.

Monday March 9	Weather too bad at Gander to start . . . all lakes frozen except Lake Gander. Went over to American Mess after dinner and had first taste of Bourbon.

Then flying conditions improve, and the diary's mood perceptibly alters.

Tuesday March 10	Left Gander at 6.45 pm . . . good flight to Montreal. Airport brilliantly lighted. Stayed at Ritz-Carlton Montreal and went over to Chateau to have a drink with AOC-in-C before turning in.
Thursday March 12	Dined with Joan Parry. Also Norah Crofton and Count de Rosieres. Went over to C-in-C for bridge. Afterwards, de Rosiers took us to Samovar.
Friday March 13	Took Elizabeth and her Canadian girl friend to El Morocco.

Reggie keeps his diary mainly as a social record. He is meanwhile finding his feet as Bowhill's Senior Air Staff Officer. The assignment is to take him over much of the Americas, and will begin his association with the great and the good which would continue until war's end.

Friday March 20	Took off Dorval in Liberator for Bermuda. Stayed Belmont Manor Hotel.
Saturday March 21	At Bermuda. Lunched Admiral Kennedy Purvis and in afternoon toured island with Flag Lieutenant and Mrs Adels in Commander Hickey (USN)'s car. Fairman's cocktail party at Belmont.

Sunday March 22	At Bermuda. Lunched HE (Lord Knollys), AVMs Midhurst and Havens there on way back to UK in Clipper. Also Rear Admiral James (USN) and Brigadier Strong (US). James took me out to his house where I dined. Good party.

The change from gloomy, wintry, rationed, combat-tense command in Scotland to the expensive, warm, safe island could not have been more dramatic, but Reggie takes it all in his stride. On return to Dorval, he dines with Air Chief Marshal Bowhill.

In April, a short visit to Washington. Back in Dorval, he notes briefly his encounters with visitors whose names underline the importance placed on the role of Ferry Command.

Tuesday April 28	Expected Dr. E.V. Evatt, Australian Minister of State for Foreign Affairs, and Mr W.S. Robinson from New York, but they did not arrive, so dined with C–in–C and Sir Kennedy Lee, the Chairman of the Maritime Commission for Industry and Export in Washington.
Wednesday March 29	Lunched in the cafeteria with C–in–C, Lady Bowhill, Mr Winant, US Ambassador to UK, and Admiral Stark USN, Mrs Winant and two other ladies.

(Admiral H.R. Stark was Commander United States Naval Forces in Europe).

And so the diary continues until June, after which affairs of greater moment than recording social and travel highlights take a higher priority in Reggie's mind.

'At Bermuda – Hilborn gave luncheon party at Ace of Clubs, Hamilton, for Tucker and self to meet Admiral James and other Bermuda notables . . .'

'At Bermuda – lunched with HE (Lord Knollys) at Government House and discussed service matters . . . tea with Admiral Sir Kennedy Purvis in Admiralty House . . . Dined with Admiral Jules James, USN – a big party . . .'

'At Jamaica – visited Palisadoes Naval Air Station and inspected RAFFC accommodation and personnel. Luncheon at Government House with HE (Sir Arthur Richards) – taken there by Captain in Charge, Captain Ringrose Wharton, RN. Cocktail party at Palisadoes p.m. and United Nations dinner at Myrtle Bank. A big show . . .'

'At Trinidad – went to RN Camp at Golden Grove (Captain Burton). Lunched at Government House – HE, Mrs Huggins, and Vice Admiral Sir Michael Hodges. Dined Government House and played bridge with HE, Mrs Huggins, and AOC . . .'

'At Dorval – the Governor General, Lord Athlone, landed with Military and Air OCs. Had tea with him in C-in-C's office . . . Liberator from Prestwick landed with Air Marshals Philip Bobington and Garrard and AVM Hollinghurst and two Group Captains . . ."

'Flew to Ottawa with C-in-C, Lady Bowhill and Powell for Governor General's Reception . . .'

'From San Francisco to Los Angeles. Landed Santa Barbara. Met by Arthur Marix and gave interview to Press. Arthur gave large cocktail party . . .'

(Colonel Arthur T. Marix was Reggie's cousin. He lived to become the oldest surviving officer of the United States Marine Corps, and was at one time President of the US Retired Officers' Association.)

'Flew to Ottawa for conference with Harold Balfour and Minister for Transport at House of Commons about TCA and Atlantic Ferry . . .'

'Louis Mountbatten, Colonel Donovan and party arrived en route for the United Kingdom . . .'

Great names planning great events. Bowhill must have relied heavily on Reggie to co-ordinate the activities of Ferry Command like a great net cast over the western hemisphere. The people he met during a hectic year as Senior Air Staff Officer were a kind of *Who's Who* of British Commonwealth and American VIPs.

Yet Reggie had known the heat of battle too intimately to be entirely satisfied with being so distant from the scenes of immediate action.

In a letter to his old school dated July 30 1942 he wrote:

'. . . I am Air Officer in charge of administration of this outfit which is a very interesting one, although *too far away from killing Germans to really please me* (italics added). But life is very pleasant and except for a quite generous rationing of petrol there is the Plenty of Peace in all directions. Also the Canadians are very hospitable and easy to get on with.

'I have done quite a bit of flying and have visited Newfoundland, Labrador, Iceland, Washington, Bermuda, Jamaica, Trinidad, Los Angeles and San Francisco . . .'

The letter revealed a certain nostalgia for his earlier days of direct, down and dirty combat – the days of Dusseldorf, of Flanders, of Aalesund. But at the same time as he was becoming familiar with every Government House from Bermuda to Trinidad, with every Colonial Secretary and Governor, he knew that Ferry Command was a war-winner. He accepted his 'safe' war, and devoted himself to the continuing success of that Command.

Even though his service as Bowhill's right-hand-man did not put him in the middle of the fighting, the value of his contribution to RAFFC during that time was recognised:

> By the KING's Order the name of
> Air Commodore R.L.G. Marix, C.B., D.S.O.,
> Royal Air Force
> was published in the *London Gazette* on
> 11 June, 1942
> as mentioned in a Despatch for distinguished service.
> I am charged to record
> His Majesty's high appreciation.
>
> (Archibald Sinclair)
> Secretary of State for Air

We do not have a record of the episode which lay behind this mention, but it reveals that Reggie's dedication to duty was every bit as strong in distant Dorval as it had been in two wars in Europe.

★   ★   ★

By 1943 the war had expanded to affect most of the globe – South-East Asia, North Africa, Europe, the Atlantic, the Mediterranean, the Pacific, all were now theatres of operations. This expansion increased the demand for air transport as the need for vital supplies, communications, airlift of personnel, ferrying of new aircraft, grew in concert with the spread of hostilities. The Royal Air Force was called upon to meet this growing demand.

Its response was to set up a world-wide Transport Command. It was created in the spring of 1943, and Air Chief Marshal Sir Frederick Bowhill was appointed as its Air Officer C-in-C.

This created a vacancy at the top of Ferry Command. The way it was filled is best described by quoting from a Canadian press report, printed under a fine profile portrait of Reggie Marix:

TAKES OVER BIG WAR JOB
RAF TRANSPORT CHIEF HERE PIONEER OF AIR AND SEA WAR

Bowhill's Successor Fought in 1914-18 and Outwits Hun in Present Conflict

Air Vice Marshal R.L.G. Marix, CB, DSO, had been appointed to the command of No. 45 (Atlantic Transport) Group of the Royal Air Force Transport Command, with headquarters at Montreal Airport, Dorval, in succession to Air Chief Marshal Sir Frederick Bowhill, GBE, KCB, CMG, DSO, who has been named Air Officer Commanding-in-Chief, RAF Transport Command, with headquarters in England.

Announcement of the appointment was made yesterday by Sir Frederick Bowhill, in a statement in which he referred to the establishment of the Ferry Command headquarters in Montreal in July, 1941, and later on at Montreal Airport, Dorval, by permission and courtesy of the Canadian Government.

The statement continues:

'On the formation of the Royal Air Force Transport Command the RAF Ferry Command will cease to exist and from 11th of April 1943 the former Ferry Command will become No 45 (Atlantic Transport) Group comprising No. 112 North Atlantic Wing and No. 113 South Atlantic Wing. It will be commanded by Air Vice Marshal R.L.G. Marix, CB, DSO.'

Reggie was now in full command of the organisation that was to continue bringing an ever-increasing flow of aircraft and material from America to Europe and North Africa. He was the ideal man for the job. Vastly experienced – thirty-one years had gone by since he had first qualified as a pilot; an outstanding 'people person', generating personal warmth and professional respect; a hard-working and exceptionally capable administrator; and – particularly important in Canada's province of Quebec – bilingual in English and French.

He was to run this vast and complex enterprise with panache, gusto, and success for more than two years – until, in fact, the Nazi machine had been beaten into rubble and chaos.

When he took over command, he was of course already a known quantity. As was his style, he hit the ground running, and was received by the Canadian public and by his Service and civilian colleagues with great enthusiasm. The mood of his reception is best spelled out by the *Montreal Standard* of 17 April 1943. At the risk of repetition of some of his story, it bears printing in full to give a flavour for the high regard in which he was held:

MAN OF THE WEEK
ATLANTIC TRANSPORT CHIEF

Air Vice Marshal Reginald L.G. Marix, CB, DSO, new head of the greatest trans-oceanic aircraft delivery service in the world, has an imposing lists of 'firsts' to his credit in air warfare, as well as in the growth of military aviation science.

Air officer commanding the Atlantic Transport Group, successor to the Royal Air Force Ferry Command, Air Vice Marshal Marix was one of the first two RNVR officers to be accepted for the naval wing of the Royal Flying Corps when it was formed 31 years ago. He carried out what was probably the first effective dive-bombing attack in military history. He was awarded the Distinguished Service Order in the first Navy honours list in the First Great War. He helped to make and drop the first depth charges ever released from an aircraft.

That's the man who is taking the place of Sir Frederick Bowhill, who steps from Commander-in-Chief of the RAFFC to occupy a similar post with the newly formed world-wide Transport Command, under which the Atlantic Transport group now operates.

Fiftyish, of medium height and fair hair, Marix has those steady 'airman's eyes'. His colleagues say he has one consuming passion – the RAF. He has no other hobbies or recreations, to their knowledge. He exemplifies everything the RAF stands for.

HARD WORKER

The AOC of the new group is slim and keeps in fine physical condition. He has that reserve which distinguishes all senior RAF officers, but his sense of humour – that subtle, dry English humor – is second to none out at Dorval airport where he makes his headquarters.

Men who have worked with him say that under pressure Marix operates at terrific spells of duty, without showing signs of fatigue. His tip-top physical shape – notwithstanding injuries from a flying accident in France, 27 years ago – keeps him going.

When you speak with Air Vice Marshal Marix, he appears extremely grave, then suddenly his face lights up and the gravity melts into a friendly smile.

Between wars, Marix made an extensive study of the possibilities of a great air war at sea, and is one of the world's great authorities on this phase of warfare, now at its climax in the Battle of the Atlantic.

The new AOC is not overly fond of public speaking. However, as senior officer of the important plane ferrying service, he will not doubt be in demand by service clubs and other organizations just as Sir Frederick Bowhill was. French-Canadians will be pleased, too, to know that Air Vice Marshal Marix has a fluent command of the French language, thanks to his education at Dieppe, Fescants, and the Sorbonne after completing his public school education at Radley.

Son of the late Mr and Mrs James Marix, Reginald Lennox George Marix was born 17 August, 1989.

A Londoner by birth, he began his service career in 1909 with the London division of the Royal Naval Volunteer Reserve. In 1912, when the Navy's flying arm was formed, he became one of the first two officers to be accepted for this branch of the service.

He learned to fly and received his Aero Club certificate at Larkhill, the same field and under the same instructors, and even at the same time, as Sir Frederick Bowhill. A few months later, he graduated as a service pilot from the Central Flying School – popularly called 'The University of the Air' – and was posted to the great

Royal Naval Air Station at Eastchurch, Essex. At the outbreak of war, he went to Dunkirk, with a naval flight attached to the Belgian Army.

AWARDED THE DSO

Early in October 1941, five weeks after the BEF had landed in France, Marix performed a brilliant feat of offensive aviation which gained for him the Distinguished Service Order in the first naval honors list of the war.

It was when Antwerp fell that Marix, flying a Sopwith Tabloid single-seater, went out from an airfield near that city to raid the Dusseldorf airship sheds. He carried out what was probably the first successful dive-bombing assault by dropping two 20-pound bombs and destroying one of the Zeppelins which in the early days of the war were seriously harassing the Allies and threatening Britain's home security.

His little plane was badly shot up, its rudder jammed, and on the return to its base ran out of gas. Landing inside the enemy sector of Antwerp, Marix boarded a locomotive hauling a train of refugees, and made his way to the city proper. He found Antwerp virtually deserted and finding a bicycle he pedalled his way out to his aerodrome. Only four or five officers remained there, and together with young Marix they escaped by car to Bruges and Ostend, where Marix rejoined his commanding officer.

After participating in the first battle of Ypres, Marix took part in the Gallipoli landing, flying over the Cape Helles sector. In that theatre of war he made good use of home-made explosives on sea targets, which were probably the first depth charges ever dropped from the air.

SERVED IN FRANCE

Called back by the Admiralty from the Dardanelles campaign towards the end of 1915 he joined the newly-formed No. 3 Canadian wing of the Royal Naval Air Service as a squadron commander. Later this wing served with outstanding success in air attacks on Germany from Luxeuil in southern France.

Marix suffered serious injuries in 1916 when he was hurt in a flying accident in France while test-flying a new French fighter plane which had just arrived from the factory.

On his recovery he served on staff duties until the end of the war, with some service at Malta. He was twice mentioned in dispatches and received the order of the Crown of Belgium.

At the outbreak of war in September 1939 Air Vice Marshal Marix was air officer commanding N. 16 group of the RAF Coastal Command which was responsible for air warfare at sea and over enemy-occupied territory from the east and southeast coasts of England.

The following year he was a member of the air staff at Coastal Command headquarters until his appointment as Air Officer commanding No. 18 group of the command, operating from northern England and Scotland. While commanding the latter group he flew on raids over the Norwegian coast. He was made a Companion of the Bath for his service with the Coastal Command.

He joined Sir Frederick Bowhill at Dorval about a year ago as air officer in charge of administration.

★   ★   ★

It was a warm welcome from the Canadian press and public.

The *Standard*'s predictions were fulfilled: he was much in demand as a speaker at all manner of functions, from Air Cadets to
Rotary meetings. His ability to switch from English to French
was a big advantage in French-speaking Montreal, where the
two language groups did not always share exactly the same
opinions and views.

As a senior figure in wartime Canada, he played a major role
in ensuring that civilian and service people were able to work
smoothly together in the common cause. To mix two meta-
phors, he was oil on troubled waters, and at the same time he
was the cement holding people together. A diplomat, in short,
using his mastery of personal relations to help keep the home
front calm while delivering the goods to completely disrupt the
enemy.

All was not figurehead appearances at public functions, however. 45 Group was a massive undertaking. Co-ordinating liter-
ally thousands of flights; bringing back ferry crews from their
trans-Atlantic destinations; organising huge numbers of ground
staff to service and prepare aircraft; liaising between all manner
of government, civilian and service people: all this and more,
with the additional challenges posed by the hazards of war.

His travelling on the business of keeping the Group in opera-
tion was global. He kept a register of no fewer than ninety-nine
airports that he visited while with Ferry Command and then the
Group – from Iceland's Reykjavik to West African Accra, from
Rio de Janeiro to Sydney's Mascot airport, from the Azores to
New Zealand, from Prestwick to Venezuela. He was the peri-
patetic managing director of a major airline – Group 45,
Limited – and a roving ambassador for Atlantic Transport.

★   ★   ★

Soon after Reggie had taken up his appointment to Ferry
Command in 1942, the war began to take a turn for the better.

Gradually the U-boat menace was overcome, the Japanese started to be rolled back in the Pacific, the North African campaigns after El Alamein went to the advantage of the Allies, the Russians moved on to the offensive. With D-day on June 6 1944 the end was in sight, even though many months of bitter fighting were still ahead.

On 8 May 1945 – 'V–E Day' – the war in Europe ended with the unconditional surrender of Germany. Hitler's Third Reich was in ruins; Hamburg, Dresden, Cologne, Essen, and most of its major cities had been devastated by the heavy aircraft of Bomber Command and the US Air Force. Great numbers of these aircraft had come from America, through the efforts first of Ferry Command and then of 45 Group. Although Germany had not been hurried into economic collapse as the proponents of strategic bombing had predicted, the destruction was awesome in its scale and had played its part in the victorious outcome.

Although Hiroshima and Nagasaki were three months in the future, and Japan would not surrender until 2 September, 45 Group's job was done. On June 15, Reggie's service record shows that he was assigned to 'Headquarters, Transport Command, Air Officer Commanding supernumerary pending posting.'

1931. In an amphibian aircraft arriving at Calshot from Hendon with 'fateful despatches from Chief of Air Staff.'

Air Vice Marshal R. Marix 1943. Commanding No. L15 Group HQ, Montreal, engaged in Atlantic Ferry and Transport.

L. to R. General Charles de Gaulle, Major Raynault, Reggie and Air Vice Marshal A. Raymond.

Reggie and Helen, Plaza Hotel, New York. 10 November 1955.

Chapter Fifteen

Close of an Era, Close of a Career

The ending of the Second World War, the awful spectre of Hiroshima and Nagasaki ushering in the nuclear age, and the rapid freeze in East-West relations which heralded the Cold War marked as abrupt a realignment of the world's hopes and fears as anything to be found in history. The certainties of Victorian England, of *Pax Britannica*, during which Reggie Marix had been brought up, were with utter finality dissolved in the mushroom cloud of the atomic bomb.

The change had not happened overnight. Reggie's inspired use of the primitive Sopwith over Dusseldorf was, in hindsight, a forerunner of the mighty air armadas over Germany and of the carrier-launched battles of the Pacific. It took two global conflicts to advance military technology to the point where man's natural aggressiveness could truly spell doom for the entire planet.

During his thirty-six years of service, from this enrolment in the Royal Naval Volunteer Reserve in 1909 to the disappearance of the need for his Atlantic Transport Group, Reggie had been an intrinsic part of an era. It had been an era in which the attrition of two global wars had reduced Britain from the status of world power sans pareil to that of a nation of the second rank, the seeds for the dissolution of empire already sown. An era in which the basic chivalry of conflict had been replaced by a

136

Clausewitzian doctrine of war as the total, all-encompassing use of raw force to achieve political ends – a regression from Reggie's return of von Lersner's sword to the Hitler-ordered shooting of recaptured RAF escapes. The close of an era indeed.

It was also the end of Reggie's years of unremitting service to the Royal Air Force.

Air Marshal Sir John C. Slessor, KCB, DSO, MC, had been appointed chief of Coastal Command in April 1943, shortly before Reggie had assumed full responsibility for Atlantic Transport. As a fellow officer in Coastal, he must have been very conscious of Reggie's reputation and of the contribution he had made to the war effort. On 20 June 1945, as Air Member for Personnel, it fell to him to write a sad personal letter to Reggie:

> Air Ministry
> Adastral House
> Kingsway WC2

Air Vice Marshal R.L.G. Marix, CB, DSO
Headquarters
Ferry Command

Dear Marix,

You will, I am sure, understand that with the end of the war against Germany we are inevitably faced with a very substantial contraction in the strength of the Royal Air Force, with a consequential reduction in the establishment of senior officers' posts. We have therefore had to review most carefully the list of officers filling vacancies on the war establishment in the ranks of Group Captain and above, and it is my unhappy task to have to give you advanced warning that your name is included in the rather long list of officers who have given long and devoted service to the RAF, but who we must now ask to be ready in the near future to retire in order to meet the contraction of establishment and make way for younger officers.

The list of officers now approved for retirement includes those who must go to bring our strength down to the estimated establishments as at July, 1946; we shall therefore have to call upon you to retire at some date before then – in your case probably within the next six months. You will of course receive a formal letter of notification, I hope you will give me as much warning as possible. I shall be sending out the formal notification approximately three months in advance which will enable you to take your leave entitlement pending retirement.

You may rest assured that we shall do our best, should you so desire, to help you find appropriate employment after retirement. Air Commodore A.H. Wann, in my department, will be available to advise you; and we have experienced RAF Liaison Officers in the London Appointments Office for ex-regulars maintained by the Ministry of Labour who, by agreement to avoid undesirable competition, have taken over the functions formerly undertaken by the RAF Officers Employment Association of pre-war days.

The oldest members of the Service will always remember you with affection as one of the foundation members and one of the first men to bomb a target in Germany. Many more will have happy memories of you in this war and will particularly associate you with the various Coastal Groups which you have commanded and with which your name will always be linked.

I do not know what you wish to do or where you intend to live after your retirement. But I know you will wish to continue your long association with the Service for which you have done so much, and hope we may be able to call on you to help us in an honorary capacity in connection with some of the many activities – such as the ATC, the RAF Association and the Benevolent Fund – in which retired officers can be of such value to the RAF and to the men who served in it.

Yours sincerely
J C Slessor

Slessor must have found that a very difficult letter to write. Reggie's stock stood high – not only for his service in the war which had just ended, but for his remarkable exploits in 1914–1918 and for the fact that he was a true founder-member of Britain's youngest armed service.

As Slessor had promised, more formal notification was on its way. Dated 31 July 1945, the letter came from the office of the Under-Secretary of State for Air, again on Air Ministry stationery:

Air Vice-Marshal R L G Marix, CB, DSO

Sir,

1   I am commanded by the Air Council to inform you that it is their policy gradually to replace senior officers in order to maintain a sufficient flow of promotion through the higher ranks, and in pursuance of this policy, they regret that it will be necessary to place you on the retired list.

2   In accordance with the provisions of Air Ministry Order A.593/45, you will be granted the same period of terminal leave with pay and allowances, as is provided in the Release Regulations for officers released in Class 'A',

i.e. 56 days, plus one day's leave for each completed month of overseas service since the 3rd September, 1939.

3   I am to confirm that there is no objection to your spending the whole or part of your terminal leave in Canada, and I am to say that if you decide to do so, your retirement will take effect 56 days, plus the amount of overseas service leave to which you may be entitled, from the date of this letter.

4   The Council have granted you permission to retain the rank of Air Vice-Marshal under the terms of Air Ministry Order A.627/41.

5   There is certain regulational information which has to be conveyed to you in connection with your retirement but this will form the subject of a separate letter.

I am, Sir, your obedient Servant . . .

The quaintness of the archaic 'your obedient Servant' has a certain wry charm in the light of the letter's content. Charming or not, it rang down the curtain on a career . . . an on an era.

Two shafts of light illuminate what must have been a gloomy period in Reggie's life.

The first was the award of the Order of Polonia Restituta, conferred on him by the President of the Republic of Poland on 12 June 1945. Polish airmen had flown alongside British for most of the war; they had played a heroic part in the Battle of Britain, and in all that ensued in the air war. The award represented a recognition of the vital role of the RAF in rolling back Nazi aggression and freeing Poland from the horrors of German occupation.

The other was a simple letter written to Reggie on July 23, 1945, by Sir Gordon Latham, KCMG, the Governor of British Guiana. It summed up the feelings of so many of his good friends:

My dear Marix,

I have been so grieved to hear that you will be retiring shortly and that I can no longer expect your pleasant company down here or at Dorval. I very well know what a good job you have been doing and I am sorry you cannot go on with it much longer, as I hear. I owe you and the Service many thanks and shall have a very good memory of the RAF Ferry Command.

However I hope you are in for a very good time indeed wherever it is that you are going off to, and I am quite sure you will make it your business to enjoy life.

With very many good wishes, believe me

Sincerely yours
Gordon Latham

Reggie's departure was a sad time for all of those who had served or worked with him through two world wars and two decades of peace. But he was able to look back upon a career which had been unrivalled in terms of spanning a period of breathtaking change. From Bleriot to B29s, he had more than lived through it all: he had been an integral part of it.

Nearly fifty-six years of age, he had given thirty-six of those years to the Service he loved. He left the Royal Air Force with his body still suffering from the damage of 1916, but with his spirit intact. In the glow of universal respect for his principles, his standards, and his achievements, it was time for him to get on with the rest of his life.

★   ★   ★

Chapter Sixteen

Retirement Years

Reggie took the Air Ministry at its word, and elected not to return to England. He had a flat in Bishop Street, Montreal, which he kept on, but often visited Nassau, Bahamas. He had the entrée to so many high-ranking people's homes that he was able to find a warm welcome almost anywhere he chose to go.

In Nassau, Sir Harold Christie – an old friend of Reggie's, and now chairman of Bahama Airways – asked him to become the honorary secretary of the Emerald Beach Club. His fame as a raconteur, warm personality, and *bon viveur* had gone before him, and he was on friendly and informal terms with the Governor, Sir William Murphy. Some time later, he attended a levée at Government House, which turned out to be a disaster of the first rank – poor planning and worse execution, all carried out by the Governor's private secretary, a civilian with no experience of protocol.

Sir William personally apologised to Reggie. 'I'm so sorry about the dreadful muddle that this levée has been. It's quite obvious that I need an ADC with a military background. You've only recently retired from the Air Force – do you know of any young officer who would like to come out here?'

It so happened that his son Nigel, who had been flying through the war, had been grounded by an ear problem that the specialists were unable to put right. Even as this conversation was going on, he was staying at his mother's flat in London undergoing innumerable tests on the damaged ear at the Central Medical Establishment.

'My son's passing the time in his mother's flat and at the Royal Air Force Club in London right now,' Reggie replied. 'It's quite obvious that he's going to be transferred to a non-flying branch. I'll ask him to come out, if you like.'

Sir William jumped at the chance, but Reggie cautioned him that it would not be easy to arrange passage for Nigel. In those post-war days there was only one service a week, in converted bombers flying for British Airways. The queues were long, with high priority going to senior government people trying to get their families back after years of absence.

The Governor had an answer for that problem. 'I will arrange things with Whitney Straight,' he said. Whitney Straight was a famous American who was head of British Airways; he had been a Royal Air Force Air Commodore.

A telegram was sent to Nigel, instructing him to go for an interview at the Colonial Office. When this was successfully completed, he went to see Whitney Straight, and by the spring of 1948 he was on his way to be ADC to the Governor of the Bahamas.

Nigel held that post for a year, when the time came for the Governor to retire. The RAF had confirmed that his ear was permanently damaged, and that he would be switched to the secretarial branch. This would have taken him away from the active aviation side of things, and he knew from watching the progress of officers who had been put into a lower medical category that promotion would be drearily slow.

What was more, Nigel sensed the changes that had occurred in the Royal Air force during the war years. 'Trenchard's Air Force' was gone, and in its place was the technocratic structure of the jet age. He knew that he would be happier outside this new and different service than in it. Luck came to his help.

In mid-1949, just as Sir William was due to retire, Sir Harold
Christie offered Nigel the job of manager of Bahama Airways.
Reggie gave good advice to his son.

'This is a fine opportunity – you're in the right place at the
right time. Why go back to England? With your ear problem,
there's no point in staying on in the service. The New World is
a good place to be, now that we are in the wonderful days of
peace.'

Nigel took his father's advice. Sir Harold sent Nigel across to
Florida to start the first international service between Palm
Beach and Nassau. The service was to be provided by flying
boats and amphibians. Although Nigel had originally been in
fighter-bombers, his ear problem had caused him to convert to
the low-altitude flying boats, so he was completely *au fait* with
the techniques of handling these very different aircraft.

In the late 1940s small airlines had a delightfully old-fashioned air about them. Reggie was fascinated to see the Bahama
Airways operation – in Coastal Command so much of his time
had been with amphibious aircraft that the sight of them flying
on civilian routes always captured his imagination.

When the airline's services had been running for some time,
Reggie had booked a trip from Nassau to Hope Town, on one
of the Out Islands. Nigel was on board as well, and was waiting
patiently in the flying boat at its dock for his father to arrive for
the 9 a.m. take-off. Father and son had been asked to stay the
weekend at the home of Rosita Forbes, the well-known American author, who had a home in the islands.

But Reggie had been up till four in the morning, gambling at
the Casino Club, following in *his* father's gaming footsteps. By
nine o'clock there was no sign of him. With all the other
passengers on board, Nigel went forward to have a word with
the captain, an American pilot called Jimmy Sproule.

'I see that your father hasn't shown up.' Jimmy was looking
down the passenger list.

'Cast off anyway, Jimmy,' Nigel said. 'I have the responsibility of managing this airline, and I can't have aircraft delayed just because my father hasn't turned up.'

'We can't leave without the Air Marshal – it just wouldn't be right. I'm going to wait for another few minutes.'

'As manager, I say that you should leave. But as captain of the aircraft, I suppose you have the final say.'

Just when Nigel was getting ready to override Sproule and get him to take off without Reggie, a car arrived on the dock alongside the flying boat. Nigel's father was in it, bleary-eyed and looking very much the worse for wear after his night at the casino. He had been staying with Colonel Freddie Wanklyn, an old Royal Flying Corps friend from First World War days, who now lived on the island in a beautiful house.

Freddie had driven him to the dock, because there was no car available for Reggie's technique of one-legged driving. They got him out of the car, bundled him and his suitcase down through the narrow hatch and into his seat. Nigel gave Captain Sproule the go-ahead, and they immediately cast off, lumbered over the smooth stretch of Bahamian water, and became airborne.

The flying boar was an old Commodore biplane of late twenties vintage – so old in fact that Nigel had offered it to the Smithsonian in Washington. He had received a reply from them which said thank you very much, but we have had one already for five years, and we are amazed that yours is still flying! In those days it was still possible for offshore airlines to get away with airworthiness standards which would not have met American or British criteria.

The ancient aircraft had clawed its way half way to Abaco Island when Jimmy left the flying to his co-pilot, came back aft and spoke to Reggie, still red-eyed and gloomy. 'Would you like to take the controls, Air Marshal? Nigel has told me that you were a flying boat pilot.'

Reggie was feeling lousy, but this was an offer he couldn't refuse. He made his way to the pilot's seat, and took over. Jimmy Sproule told his co-pilot to go back, and installed Nigel in his seat. The young co-pilot – new to the airline, and unaware that Nigel himself was an experienced flying boat captain – took a look at the one legged man at the controls and at his boss in the right hand seat, gulped, turned quite pale, and retreated into the main cabin with a look of grave concern on his face.

Jimmy was an ex-USAF fighter pilot, skilful and cool-nerved, but without the air of steadiness and responsibility that usually goes with the average airline captain. He followed his co-pilot to the back of the aircraft, flopped into a vacant seat, and began reading a men's magazine.

He had assumed that Nigel knew the islands. But he didn't know this particular one, and what's more Jimmy had failed to indicate their whereabouts on the chart. But father and son pressed on into the unknown. They both roared with laughter when, as they checked their instruments, the airspeed indicator hand suddenly went from 80 to zero, shaken off its spindle by the vibration of the old flying boat.

Reggie asked his son if he could see Hope Town. 'No,' replied Nigel. 'But looking at the time, I think we must have passed it!'

So Nigel left his co-pilot's seat, and went back to where Jimmy Sproule was still engrossed in his lurid magazine and the authentic co-pilot was sitting, white-knuckled, gazing at a container on the bulkhead marked SHARK REPELLENT.

Nigel raised his voice to overcome the vibrating roar in the cabin. 'Jimmy, I think we've gone way past Hope Town.' He was heard by all the startled passengers around him, well-behaved and rather formal north-easterners visiting the mid-season Bahamas.

'Have we?' Sproule didn't look up from the page. Then he reluctantly climbed his way out of the seat, and followed Nigel back to the flight deck. 'Oh, yes,' he said, when he had a good view of the waters ahead, 'we've overflown all right. We'll have to do a 180 and head back the way we've come.'

'Well, for God's sake get my father out of there, take command yourself, and aim for where we're meant to be going.'

The controls were exchanged, and the aircraft went into a steep banking turn as the one-legged Reggie made his way from the flight deck, the genuine co-pilot pushed past him, and Nigel followed his father. Not given to panic, the formal Bostonians looked rather bewildered as this game of airborne musical chairs was enacted before them.

It did not take Jimmy Sproule long to get on to a reciprocal course, sniff out their destination, and put the old aircraft down into the water slowly and gently. A dinghy came alongside and the passengers – still slightly dazed, unable to believe that what they had seen had really happened – were transferred safely ashore.

Reggie and Nigel enjoyed their weekend with Rosita Forbes.

★   ★   ★

Such was the stuff of those post-war years. In some ways they were evocative of Malta in the 'thirties; social, light-hearted, climatically pleasant, but without the exigencies of the service hanging over either father or son.

Reggie made a few forays into business life, but in sharp contrast to his Air Force career they were uniformly unsuccessful. He lost a lot of money in gold shares, having made bad investments on the advice of some Canadian friends. He got into the paint business; the idea was to get contracts for paint purchases for use by civilian and military ships, using his many contacts in naval and mercantile shipping circles. But again, this didn't work out.

He put his inventive powers to work, and came up with a compass ring, a ring which could be worn on the finger, and which contained a north-seeking needle. The concept was fine. With no separate piece of equipment to carry, trekkers, backwoodsmen, American hunters in the great forests of the north would have a simple way of direction finding. The idea came to grief in translation to production, and it never became a viable proposition.

Like so many service officers after a career of dedication to their country, he lacked the business acumen to recognise all the pitfalls in commerce. Other, more perspicacious, business people were very ready to take advantage of his inventive brain and his wide range of contacts, but his own enterprises did not bring him financial success.

Despite these disappointments, he was able to continue maintaining his pleasant Montreal flat, where he spent the summer months. In the winters – 'the season', in the Bahamas – he was happier enjoying the climate of Nassau. Sometimes he would rent an apartment there, but more often he was the house guest of wealthy residents for a month or more at a time. War hero and great social asset, he was ever popular in the homes of his friends and acquaintances. His life in retirement was full and enjoyable.

Just one thing was missing. Without a wife to share his retirement years, he was becoming lonely.

By the 1950s he had been unmarried for thirty years – Pixie and he had been divorced in 1924. That event had left a scar on his soul which had until now inhibited him from even thinking of remarriage. He had relied on Pixie a great deal. He had been desperately hurt when she had left him for another man, more so than a man with a whole body would have been.

But there were always women in his life. Rich women, young women, beautiful women. Even if not at the deep level of making a commitment to marriage, he never lacked for female companionship. In the inter-war years, he was able to devote himself to his profession, but at the same time to enjoy a lively, even hectic, social life. Sometimes that social life was in London's Mayfair, when he was desk-bound at the Air Ministry, and sometimes in even more hectic Malta. He was a wonderful, thoughtful host, an accomplished entertainer, an asset to any party.

During the war years, his dedication while in Coastal Command was complete, and fun and games were not on his agenda. In Canada, however, he was able to enjoy a degree of relaxation; although his responsibilities were demanding indeed, the pressures of warfare did not weigh upon his command.

In Canada he came as close as he had since he and Pixie had parted to forming a real romantic attachment. Maddy Rodier was her name. They were very fond of each other, and he kept a photograph of her in his album of those wartime Canadian years. But she was already married to a Wing Commander. Reggie could not have brought himself to commit what he would have seen as an act of betrayal of someone in his own service; neither would he have been able to inflict on another man the sort of hurt he had suffered himself twenty years earlier. Had he thought otherwise, and felt that he could weather the storm of being the cause of a messy and dramatic divorce, she would have married him at once. She adored him. Instead, their closeness remained a friendship to be treasured, but take no further.

After the war, in his early retirement years, he was constantly being asked by his concerned friends 'Reggie, why don't you marry so-and-so? She's crazy about you – what's more, she's a multi-millionairess!' His standard reply was: 'Well, she simply doesn't spin my motors!'

He could never bring himself to marry for money. In the 1930s, the years of the Great Depression, service pay had been reduced, so that even if he had met a lady with whom he could overcome his inhibitions about marriage, he would not have had a lot of money to offer a prospective bride. He was already on first name terms with some very wealth women. But he would not lower his own standards to enter into marriage just to improve his financial situation.

By the mid 1950s his loneliness had become more acute. His admirers, male and female, were good friends, but he began to realise that there was a lot of superficiality in the constant social round. He was now 65. His willpower was strong, strong as it had ever been, but he was increasingly conscious of the encroaching signs of age. He had already experienced some minor heart trouble. With these intimations of mortality added to his long-time disability, he felt more and more alone in the world. He needed permanent companionship.

In short, he needed a wife.

At this critical juncture in his emotional life, along came Helen Holmes. They met in Nassau, on the cocktail circuit. Helen was a tall, strikingly good-looking woman, just a few years younger than Reggie. Of Hungarian extraction, she was a strong character – no stronger than Reggie himself, but certainly a match for him.

Helen was not a rich woman, although her parents had been wealthy. She was one of a big family of sisters, and had daughters of her own from a previous marriage. By the time the money had filtered down to them all, she was not left with a great deal. Even so, she maintained a Manhattan apartment and a house in Horse Neck's Lane in Southampton, New York. She was one of the very tight upper social circle of the United States.

Meeting Helen to a great extent determined the pattern of Reggie's life for his remaining years.

Clearly, they enjoyed their courtship. Helen had been married three times previously, Reggie once, but they were free of direct family responsibilities. They were able to have fun together, to look forward to their later years in each other's company.

Early in January 1955 they set off for a two-month motoring trip to Torremolinos. Reggie recorded it as a diary, along the lines of Jerome K. Jerome's *Three Men in a Boat*. The title *A Jalopy in France and Spain*.

His notes on the trip reflect their contentment and delight in being together, and the light-heartedness they both brought to their companionship. This was the way they wanted their life to be. A few of his comments give a flavour of their *joie de vivre*:

'*January 13* – I buy a Spanish dictionary, and Helen buys a bottle of scotch. We proceed towards the border when Helen thinks it wise to open the scotch because of possible Customs difficulties. We seize this opportunity to sample it. Proceed another two miles when Helen speculates whether there is still too much in the bottle. Decides that there is and takes remedial action. Proceed three miles when Helen considers it prudent to ensure that Spanish Customs will not object to amount in the bottle. Takes appropriate action. Arrive at Customs where Helen declares that we have nothing to declare but any undying love for Spain. Amid cries of '*Olé Señora!*' we are allowed to proceed without our luggage even being looked at. A little further on we decide to drink a little scotch to celebrate this diplomatic victory . . .'

'*January 15* – We got to the Ritz with the intention of having luncheon there but first go into the lounge for martinis. When the bill for these arrives I calculate that I am paying for a bottle of gin, a bottle of vermouth, an olive tree and that month's hire purchase instalment on the table and two chairs we are occupying. If the restaurant prices are comparable we shall have to raise a loan which the Banca Espanol and the American Express between them may be able finance; but first we glance into the palatial restaurant . . .'

'*January 17* – We drive to Granada, a distance of only 93 miles but decide to stay at the Parador San Francisco until tomorrow as this ancient city is full of interest. We employ a guide to show us over the magnificent Alhambra built some 800 years ago by the Moors for their Sultan. I notice that the guide gives Helen some sly looks as he points out where the Sultan and his Harem used to have their evening gin and bitters, and there was a positive leer on his face when he explained the duties of the eunuchs. I am pleased to note that Helen looks him straight in his wall eye as if she had never heard of the word . . .'

'*February* (at the Opera House, Malaga) – The opera almost defied description. Although some of the voices were quite good there obviously existed the greatest animosity between the cast and the orchestra, both of which were determined to ignore each other. They only had one point in common. Every singer and each member of the orchestra appeared to be in agreement to pay no attention whatever to the conductor. After the interval when Pagliacci began, the curtain, of course, remained down, and this was covered with gaudy advertisements depicting the various commodities obtainable in the local shops. For the Prologue the baritone chose a vivid advertisement for spring mattresses to stand in front of. The orchestra, elated by its success in having got the better of the cast in Cavalleria, went off at full speed and soon got two bars ahead of the singer. But the baritone was a man of parts and not easily to be outdone. Filling his lungs to capacity he put on such a spurt that he established a lead which he was able to maintain to the end, taking his bow while the orchestra, or at any rate most of it, was still three bars behind the finish and the exhausted conductor only half way down the score. The performance did not end until a quarter to three and I suggested going to a café for a drink, but Helen not feeling like creating a sensation two nights in succession chose to go straight home . . .'

(On leaving Malaga) – 'We have decided to return via the Mediterranean coast and make for Perpignan and Carcassonne. It will be with a heavy heart that I shall leave 'La Roca' where I have spent such a happy time . . .'

'*March 5* – We have not gone far before we have our first delay since leaving Paris. A recurrent thump gives warning that a tyre is about to blow out. Fortunately we have passed a garage about a quarter of a mile back and we are able to crawl back. The spare wheel is put on but as the damaged tyre is past repair we stop in Toulouse and buy an old used cover for a temporary spare. All this has taken time so that when we arrive at Caussade it is past 3 o'clock. We are no longer in Spain and it is well past the *déjeuner* hour. We arrive in the main square where, in the middle, a Sergeant de Ville is mounted on a dais.

Helen suggests inquiring where we can get some lunch. I know from experience in Paris, Madrid and Barcelona etc that she revels in talking to policemen, particularly when they are busy regulating the traffic, and that it would be futile to try to deter her. I pull up beside the dais and she begins with her most disarming smile: 'Pardon, Monsieur, mais nous avons été – un pneu crevé – et en conséquence . . .' and she goes on to explain in her fluent French that she knows that we are late for lunch and does Monsieur le Sergeant de Ville know of somewhere where we could get a simple 'repas'. We do not want anything 'compliqué'. Just a few hors d'oeuvres to begin with and then a plain omelette, not too well done, in fact slightly 'baveuse'. Then perhaps some 'fromage'. As for the wine: with an omelette 'c'est une question de goût' . . .

In the meantime I notice that chaos is beginning to reign. About five streets converge on the square and vehicles are rushing at each other from all directions. There are many narrow escapes from serious collision. The sergeant is quite oblivious, clearly hypnotised by Helen, and is twirling his moustaches in a most engaging fashion. Yes, he knows of the very restaurant where undoubtedly they will be satisfied. It is only when several frantic citizens scream that they have sent for the mayor that he comes for himself and attempts to unravel and traffic. With difficulty I extricate myself, drive to the restaurant the sergeant has recommended, only to find it closed. We go elsewhere . . .'

'*March 6* – We have spent four days in Paris and on the third Helen thought she ought to make arrangements for her flight to Nassau. This was not to be as simple as one might have supposed. She had flown from New York to Paris by KLM on a return ticket she had won in a quiz by a *tour de force* of musical knowledge. She now wanted to dispose of the return half, go to London and fly direct from there to Nassau by BOAC instead of going via New York. But on inquiry she was informed that her ticket, being in the nature of a prize, was non-transferable and non-negotiable. She could either use it or lose it.

Helen immediately accepted the challenge and mobilized her forces. She had in strategic reserve the American Ambassador, but decided on an attack without delay by her line of battle. Deploying the First Chase National Bank under the command of General Julian Allen (who with the whole of his staff was obliged to remain at Bank Headquarters on a half-holiday) she launched a vigorous offensive which proved decisive. The KLM forces were drawn up in the Place de l'Opéra, but after a spirited skirmish among the tables of the Café de la Paix, were routed. Pourparlers ensued and an armistice was arranged by the terms of which Field Marshal Helen was to be given a specially upholstered seat in a KLM aircraft from London to Amsterdam where she would transfer into another of the Company's aircraft with a bigger and better upholstered seat as far as Havana, via Prestwick in Scotland, and Montreal. From Havana she would have to be find her own way to Nassau which she could do by first flying to Florida. If this was not exactly a direct route, it was a victory for the Field Marshal . . .'

'*March 13* – Helen's plane leaves the London Airport (Heath Row) this afternoon and she has been asked to be there an hour before departure time. I suspect that this is to give the Movietone News and the Press a fair chance, but we think that a half hour should be enough . . . For some inexplicable reason I not only forget the distance to London but also miscalculate the position of Heath Row. After a leisurely luncheon I suggest that we should start. It is only when we are on the road that I realise how far we have to go. Fortunately it is a Sunday and there is little traffic, but I really have to keep the old jalopy moving and we have the whole breadth of London to traverse. Helen keeps calm but my blood pressure mounts for I realize that if I miss the aircraft the battle of the Place de l'Opéra will have been fought in vain. We arrive with two minutes to spare. An official is waiting and Helen is whisked away, spirited through Immigration and Customs and ushered into a large and empty bus that is waiting for her. The moment she enters the aircraft the engines are started. It has been a very close thing.

I return to the car and disconsolately drive back to London. The empty seat beside me looks very empty indeed . . .'

'Very empty indeed.' Reggie was by now in his 66th year, and did not want loneliness to be a constant companion for his retirement years. Helen was fun; she had great numbers of friends and acquaintances; she was, he felt, a complementary character to his own. Six months later, they were married, in Darien, Connecticut. The American press sensed the social nature of the event:

MRS KRECH HOLMES WED TO AIR VICE MARSHAL MARIX

Darien, Conn., Sept 15. – Announcement is made of the marriage yesterday of Mrs. Krech Holmes, of New York and Southampton, L.I., to Air Vice Marshal Reginald Lennox George Marix, of London, England. The ceremony was performed at the Darien home of Mr. and Mrs. William Ziegler by Justice of the Peace Alexander Klahr in the presence of the immediate families and a few intimate friends.

Mrs. Marix, the former Miss Helen Krech, is the daughter of the late Mr. and Mrs. Alvin Krech, of New York. She attended schools in New York and in Europe and made her debut in New York and is a member of the Colony Club. This is her fourth marriage. By her first husband, Mr. L. Stuart Wing, of Santa Barbara, Calif., she has two daughters, Mrs Samuel Fairchild, of Brookville, L.I., and Mrs Craig Mitchell, of Caracas, Venezuela, and by her second husband, Mr Phillip Cussachs, who died in 1932, another daughter, Mrs Xavier Fonsale, of Paris, France.

Her third husband was Mr. Duncan Holmes, who died in 1953.

Vice-Marshal Marix, who was educated at Radley College in England, joined the Royal Naval Air Service in 1912, served in Belgium and France in World War I and received the Order of the Crown of Belgium and the Belgium *Croix de Guerre*. He served with the Royal Air Force throughout World War II in Coastal Command and Transport Command. He retired in 1945. By his first marriage, which was dissolved by divorce, he has a son, former Squadron Leader Nigel Marix, Royal Air Force, who now lives in Palm Beach, Fla., and who was present at the wedding. Also present at the ceremony were the bride's brother, Dr Shepard Krech, of New York, and her sisters, Mrs Sheffield Cowles, of Farmington, Conn., and Mrs. Harris T. Lindeberg, of Locust Valley, L.I.

The newlyweds lived for a few months in Helen's Southampton house and in her New York apartment. But they soon made up their minds to move to a more relaxed location, a place where they could be their congenial, social selves, where the climate was warmly temperate without the subtropical heat of Nassau. To a place, in short, where the livin' was easy.

In 1956 they packed up all their worldly goods, and took an Italian liner to Majorca. Here they moved into a villa called SA SERRA – 'His Wash' – at Paguera, near Palma, and looked forward to a very pleasant married life in retirement.

In the 'fifties Majorca was not the tourist-oriented island that it was later to become. Life was as calm and quiet as one wished it to be. Inexpensive, too: a retired expatriate couple possessed of means that would not be considered flamboyant wealth in their country of origin could live in leisured style not very far short of opulence.

Reggie and Helen entertained; they had live-in staff; they ate and drank well. Life centred on the home, on meals, on the cocktail hour, on whatever cultural pursuits were available in Palma. Reggie took up his pen once more, and combined his aptitude for words with his knowledge of music to produce some very amusing pieces. He contributed this article to the *Majorca News* of 26 October 1962:

REGGIE MARIX WRITES AGAIN

The first concert of the season, given by the Symphony Orchestra under the direction of Mr Morss in the Teatro Principal on 10th October, introduced a novelty which, if further developed, might well lead to a revolution in concert presentation and place Palma de Majorca, as originator of the technique, in the forefront of that select coterie of cities, such as Salzburg, Edinburgh, and Baiphong, which are famous for their music festivals.

I refer to the bizarre and novel stage effect by which
the talented and beautiful young Dutch soprano, Mme
Yvette Noë, was placed in almost complete darkness so
that she could be seen only in silhouette while the
conductor and orchestra were clearly visible. I have seen
some singers when this stratagem would have been an
advantage, but in the case of the comely Miss Noë it
robbed the audience of much of the pleasure in listening
to her lovely voice.

Dramatic

Why not carry this technique a stage further and plunge
the whole stage into darkness during the actual performance of an item? To give full effect to this dramatic
device the stage should first be very brilliantly illumi-
nated indeed, say by a hundred Klieg lights, so that the
transition to complete darkness would be all the more
marked. This would, of course, entail careful timing.

After the assembly of the instrumentalists on the concert platform, the conductor would take his stance on
the podium, his eyes shielded by a large green visor. As
he bowed to the audience the soloist, wearing sunglasses, would enter. Then the orchestra squinting in the
violent glare (visors and sunglasses would be the pre-
rogative of conductors and guest artists) would blink
expectantly at the conductor. He would raise his baton,
make a few deceptive flourishes, bring it decisively
down and as the first resounding crash emanated from
the orchestra the master electrician would throw a
switch and both stage and auditorium would be plunged
into Stygian blackness.

Apart from artistic novelty this procedure would have
other advantages. In the same way as when blindness
afflicts a man his hearing becomes more acute, and a deaf

man can spot a pretty girl on the beach from a greater distance than an ordinary chap, so the audience's appreciation of the subtle nuances of, say, the Ride of the Valkyries, would be enhanced by not being able to see anything. Another advantage would be that the conductor, well practised in the game of 'blind man's buff' could pick his way unnoticed through the instrumentalists to the wings and enter a lighted sanctum where he could knock back a few cognacs before returning to the podium to make his bow as the lights went up at the moment of the final chord.

Avant Garde

One can anticipate a notice that might appear in the *Majorca News* on some future date after a concert.

'Last night the Symphony Orchestra of Palma, avant garde of the new technique of "Son et Ténèbres", presented a concert redolent of emotional verve. The guest conductor was the renowned Sir Beowful Tawneybotham from the London Coliseum, and the soloist, the famous Sicilian baritone, Signor Vermisilli. The performance opened with a rendition of the prologue from 'Pagliacci'. Right on the dot, that is to say, as Sir Beowulf smacked his empty music stand with his baton, all the lights were extinguished and the audience was held in ecstatic thrall as the booming voice of Signor Vermisilli introduced the opening motif.

Football

'This was the first occasion on which Sir Beowful had taken part in "Son et Ténèbres" and whereas many another conductor would have prudently quitted the podium, Sir Beowulf showed that he was made of sterner stuff. There was, perhaps, a certain want of cohe-

sion in the orchestra due to lack of rehearsals as several
of the instrumentalists had only returned from Barcelona
late that afternoon after playing in a football match . . .'

Reggie was able to combine his talent for words with his
knowledge of music, and to add to the mix a gentle irony. His
satire was never biting, his criticism never hurtful. He was able
to inform, to amuse. Sensing that the original piece had struck a
chord, he contributed a follow-up to the same journal:

A MUSICAL TREAT IN STORE

Since the publication in your issue of October 26th of
my suggestions that the Palma Symphony Orchestra
should initiate 'Son et Ténèbres' I have been bombarded
by your readers with telegrams and letters of congratula-
tion and appreciation. So great was the volume that I
had to engage two extra secretaries to deal with this
correspondence.

   These tributes, and if I may say so without boasting,
homage to my dramatic genius, encourage me to make a
further incursion into the realm of music. In the *Daily
Telegraph* of November 14th the following paragraph
appeared in the column 'Around America Today'.

   'ORCHESTRAL SHOEHORNS
   The United States premier of an orchestral work by
   Kiyoshiga Koyama which calls for nine shoehorns,
   will be given on Sunday at Evanston, Illinois, by the
   North Western Symphony Orchestra. The shoehorns
   will be drawn across the strings of the cellos, basses
   and harps: the work is called "Three Noh Masks".'

On the principle that 'what Kiyoshiga Koyama can do I
can do better', I am composing a Symphonic Fantasia in

which not a single shoehorn is used. On the other hand, in addition to the usual instruments which comprise a symphony orchestra, there will be two bugles, six inflated paper bags (to be exploded by the harpist), a silver plated ocarina, an American police car siren, three humming tops, a foghorn from a Paguera excursion boat and, last but not least, a sackful of broken glasses. Furthermore the violas will each have 25 buckshot dropped into those two curly apertures so that at appropriate moments the player can grip the bow between his teeth and shake his viola with both hands thereby producing (in a symphony) an unusual diaphonic effect. The sack of broken glasses (which can be collected during the early hours of any morning from bars in the vicinity of the Plaza Gomila) will be dropped at the perihelion of a climatic crescendo from above on to a slab of marble between the two buglers who will be allowed to wear firemen's helmets if apprehensive about the ballistics of the sack.

I must not detract from the listeners' pleasure by divulging too many of the surprises which will be incorporated in the musical 'tour de force' but, weather permitting, the score should be completed in three weeks. I will then submit it to the Impresario of the Teatro Principal, who I hope will send me two free tickets for the first performance.

The work is to be called 'Ten Little Pigs' . . .

When in Mallorca with Deedy, Nigel observed that Reggie wrote; Helen socialised. The pattern of their initially idyllic Majorcan life began to polarise round these two themes. More and more, the pleasures of wine and leisure took her into their embrace, while for him the attractions of his den and his world of writing became increasingly important. Not that he became monastic in his habits; he had always enjoyed his nightcap of whisky and soda, and wine was served with every meal. But alcohol did not assume for him the importance that it did for Helen. He bore with patience and kindness this growing imbalance between them.

Those closing years became less fulfilling than Nigel had hoped for his father. Reggie sometimes visited Palm Beach where Nigel and his wife Deedy were involved in the travel business, but on these occasions social commitments were so heavy that there was little chance of father-son talk, or indeed of informal family conversations at all. Nigel and Deedy made several visits to the Majorca establishment, but again the ebb and flow of daily events made serious discussion difficult.

While maintaining a highly 'social' attitude to life, Helen's focus on alcohol set its own agenda. Nigel remembers appearing for breakfast with Deedy at a reasonably early hour, and being joined by Reggie. But his father would not stay for long. He would retreat into his study and write, to fill in the time before Helen arose from her slumbers.

This might be at eleven or so, after the live-in maid had brought her breakfast in bed. It was the signal to repair to the end of the garden, to swim, and to partake of the wine or of martinis from a decanter which Helen had thoughtfully provided for her guests and herself.

A couple of hours of water-play and of drinking, and lo! lunchtime. Being Spain, this meant two or half past, paella and a flagon of wine on the table, and a long siesta afterwards.

The end of siesta signalled time to arise once more and to prepare for the evening's entertainment. Dining out or whatever, the inevitable drinking provided the mainstay of the night.

This pattern as it developed meant that Nigel had little opportunity to share reminiscences with his father. He was able to observe how understanding Reggie was with Helen, as she became progressively more 'difficult' because of the demon drink, and to admire him for that loving forbearance. After Reggie had confided to Nigel the situation, Nigel and Deedy regretfully ceased travelling to his father's Mediterranean home.

Chapter Seventeen

Mission Completed

The light was fading now. The years were weighing more heavily on Reggie, slowly bringing to an end a life which had conquered injury, pain, war, and heavy personal burdens.

In his seventy-seventh year, on January 7, 1966, the Air Vice Marshal died in Palma Hospital following a heart attack.

Obituaries were published in many places where Reggie Marix had been respected, admired, and loved – Great Britain, the United States, Nassau, Majorca among them. Many were abbreviated biographies, short life stories which were true enough but in the nature of things did not capture the essence of the man. A few, however, managed in just a few words to paint a more telling picture, omitting all verbiage and getting to the core of the story. The *London Times*, on 12 January 1966:

OBITUARY
AIR VICE MARSHAL R.L.G. MARIX

C.L.C. writes:-
Those of the 'First Contingent' of the flying services and probably many others will be saddened by the news of the death of Reggie Marix. Joining the original R.N.A.S. in 1912 he learnt to fly at Eastchurch and in the early days of the 1914-18 War accompanied the

redoubtable Commander Samson with a mixed force of aircraft and armoured cars in Belgium. He was one of the first to destroy a Zeppelin by bombing its shed at Dusseldorf from a very low height, an exploit for which he was awarded a well-deserved D.S.O.

He went on with Samson to the Dardanelles and took part in many bombing raids there. On being recalled home in 1915, Samson wrote in his memoirs that 'not only was he one of the finest pilots that ever was, but combined this skill with the most conspicuous gallantry and grim determination.' In 1916 an aircraft he was testing in Paris broke up in the air and the crash resulted in the amputation of his left leg thus putting an end to an active flying career. Nevertheless he remained in the Service and during the 1939-45 War reached the rank of Air Vice Marshal.

Reggie overcame his disability and severe pain with the help of a great sense of humour and many senior Naval and Air officers will remember the way in which he often succeeded in reconciling the acerbities which bedevilled inter-Service relations between the wars. As second in command of Transport Command in Canada he made a host of friends and remained there for some years after his retirement in 1945.

Other obituaries had found nuggets of information which were less well-known, but which threw interesting sidelights on his life. The *Nassau Guardian*, on 13 January:

He learned to fly in 1912 and before World War 1 made what is believed to have been one of the first social flying visits in England. He attended a lunch with his sister at Milton Villa, Little Holland, after which he flew on to a tea party at Frinton, landing in nearby fields on both occasions.

The *Guardian* went on to note that in November 1964, he attended the last formal dinner reunion of the pre-World War 1 pilots which was held at the Royal Air Force Club.

Apart from formal obituaries, Reggie's death gave rise to the publication of a number of anecdotes which added colour to the established record. The *Daily Telegraph* on 10 January:

UNFAIR TO THE BARON

Air Vice Marshal Marix, who has died at 76, not only destroyed the first Zeppelin in the 1914 by bombing its shed at Dusseldorf from 600 feet but was also the hero of another remarkable exploit.

He had to make a forced landing while on reconnaissance during the German advance on Antwerp, and learned that some British troops were being held captive at a nearby château.

Marix collected eight Marines and set out to release them. A surprised squadron of Uhlans fled, leaving behind an officer, Baron von Lersner, and his batman beside their injured horses.

The baron was furious when he discovered how small a force had routed his much bigger one. 'We thought you were the British Army,' he complained.

This one episode seemed to capture the public imagination. It gave rise to further correspondence in the *Telegraph*, perhaps because people knew instinctively that in some way the conduct of the Marix – von Lernser clash marked the end of an era, a final flowering of chivalry in its medieval sense. On 19 January H.E.P. Burns wrote to the paper:

A GENTLEMEN'S WAR

Sir – Peterborough's reference to Air Vice Marshal Marix's death at the age of 76, and his exploits in the early weeks of the 1914-1918 war, reminds me that 30 years ago we spent some pleasant evenings together in Mdina Notabile, Malta, where – as Group Captain – Marix was senior air officer.

In the incident of the clash with the German scouting Uhlans and the capture of Baron von Lernser the point which the newspapers of that day took up was that Marix handed back to the German officer his own revolver so that he could put his injured horse out of its misery.

It was a gentleman's war in the early 1914 days, at least among the professionals. We were using armoured cars, many of them naval, against which the German Uhlans had little to offer.

This called for further comment:

WAR AND PEACE

Sir – The letter which Mr H.E.P. Burns wrote to you about a conversation between myself and the late Air Vice Marshal seems to me to call for an additional comment.

The characterisation 'A Gentleman's War' not only applies to the moment when Marix gave me his revolver so that I could shoot my horse. At the same time he offered to let me keep my sword. Although this was only October, 1914, one nevertheless had the impression that it would be a long war. I therefore asked Marix to send me the sword after the war.

This he indeed did, sending me the sword through our air attaché in Berlin. The handing over was recorded in the British and German Press.

If I could say something about all the things that have happened since then, I would wish only that there should be no more war between European peoples, but

that the young generations should marshal their
thoughts under the slogan 'A Gentleman's Peace.'

Yours faithfully
W. von LERSNER
Schallstadt, Germany

Reggie's death was the subject of public record and recognition. Privately, but officially, the sorrow of the whole Royal Air Force was put into words in a letter from Sir Martin Flett, KCB, to Helen:

MINISTRY OF DEFENCE
MAIN BUILDING
WHITEHALL
LONDON SW1

11 January 1966

Madam
I am writing on behalf of the Air Force Board to express their deep regret on learning of the death of your husband Air Vice Marshal R.L.G. Marix, CB, DSO.

The Board recall with gratitude your husband's long and varied career in war and peace. He rendered gallant service during the war of 1914-18, and, whilst serving with the Royal Naval Air Service destroyed, at Dusseldorf, the first Zeppelin to be destroyed by the Allied Forces. He joined the Royal Air Force on its formation in 1918, and following a number of senior staff appointments in the succeeding years, served with distinction in the Second World War as Air Officer Commanding No. 18 Group, Air Command Canada and Headquarters Transport Group.

The Board desire me to convey to you their profound sympathy in your bereavement.

But Helen, too, died less than a year later. Even though their later married years had been less fulfilling than perhaps they had dreamed, her emotional investment in Reggie had been too great for her to carry on alone.

It was the end of an era.

Chapter Eighteen

Epilogue

Few can claim as vivid a life as that of Reggie Marix. He was a mixture of several superficially opposite characteristics. Warm and responsive to people, but at the same time self-disciplined. A party-goer and -giver when the setting was appropriate, but monastically dedicated to round-the-clock duty when his country needed him. Raconteur, pianist, hypnotist, and writer of light-hearted prose, yet never free of pain since the loss of his leg. Aware of the wider world around him, bilingual, always able to see the other chap's point of view, derisive of chauvinism . . . but committed to patriotism, to the service of his country, because he believed in a just cause.

Extraordinary in his achievements. He was an outstanding pilot in the early days of the First World War, when the average life of aircrew was measured in days, he showed what could be done by rudimentary aircraft in the strike role against the Zeppelin menace. Progress – slow at first, very slow – through the ranks into the inter-war RAF, the years that saw the Wall Street crash and the great Depression. Achievement of active Air Rank in the Second War despite a physical handicap perhaps surpassed only by that of the legendary Douglas Bader.

Looking back with the hindsight that nearly three decades can give, his character and achievements can be set more clearly against the times in which he lived. Those time can be summarised in just one word:

Change.

Change more bewildering, more global, more massive in scale than any era of history. Change which was only possible in a world that had gone through its industrial revolution, whose technology was able to change the direction of vast forces, to support even vaster conflicts, to tear down existing social structures – empires, even – in a few short years.

If one takes a quick glance back at history, events such as the signing of the Magna Carta or the upheaval of the French Revolution can be seen as almost parochial in scale. Certainly, ideas took root that would eventually come to play a part in the political shaping of today. But from a practical standpoint such events, seen as earth-shaking in their time, had little or no impact beyond their immediate surroundings, or at most the country in which they took place.

But in Reggie's time, the forces of change never ceased rumbling underfoot, at times (as in the two major wars in which he fought) breaking into destruction on a scale never before dreamt of.

The nineteenth century had been dominated by Great Britain. The Empire was the ultimate arbiter over much of the world's land surface, and most of its seas. No power could launch a successful challenge against it. Never – not even in the greatest days of Rome – had one nation commanded such vast sweeps of territory, or exercised that command with such economic and military power.

At the time of Victoria's Diamond Jubilee in 1897, the young Reggie was eight years old. This is how historian James Morris, in *Farewell the Trumpets*, sees the mood of Empire at that time:

> If there was one characteristic . . . it was an almost feverish enthusiasm. The mood of Empire in 1897 was

bravura – 'an attempt', as the painter Constable once
defined it, 'at something beyond the truth'. The British
Empire was a heady outlet for the imagination of a
people still in its prime. Its subjects were of all races: its
activists were nearly all British. Through the gate of
Empire Britons could escape from their cramped and
rainy islands into places of grander scale and more vivid
excitement, and since the Queen's accession at least 3
million had gone. By 1897 they were everywhere. There
were Britons that year commanding the private armies of
the Sultan of Sarawak, organizing the schedules of the
mountain railway to Darjeeling, accepting the pleas of
runaway slaves in Muscat, charting the China Sea, commanding the Mounties' post on the Chinook Pass in the
Yukon, governing the Zulus and the Wa, invading the
Sudan, laying telegraph wires across the Australian out-
back, editing the *Times of India*, prospecting for gold in
the valley of the Limpopo, patrolling the Caribbean and
investigating the legal system of the Sikhs – all within
the framework of Empire, and under the aegis of the
Crown.

All this the Diamond Jubilee reflected. It was . . . a
grand and somewhat vulgar spectacle, reflecting a tremendous and not always delicate adventure, and
perfectly expressing the conviction of Cecil Rhodes, the
imperial financier, that to be born British was to win
first prize in the lottery of life.

Of course, Reggie the boy could not have known this vast
expanse of Empire. But he was growing up in an environment
where its great and continuing power was unquestioned (the
size of its Navy was based on the combined size of the next two
navies in the world), and where Britannia ruled the waves. The
fact that Britannia also from time to time waived the rules was

lost in the overwhelming public support and enthusiasm for the British Empire, on which the sun never set.

This was the national atmosphere of Reggie's early years. It was not yet evident to the general public that the worm had begun to gnaw away inside the apple, although the knowledgeable knew that Germany and the United States were fast overhauling his country in technology, military strength, and economic power. The national and international barometers were set fair, but all unbeknownst to the man in the street, the needle would soon – very soon – point to change.

Change was in the air in much more immediately obvious ways. Submarines were reluctantly brought into the Navy at the turn of the century. Perhaps the twelve-year-old marvelled at the introduction of the primitive Holland class boats, invisible hunters beneath the sea. He was fourteen when the Wright Brothers achieved what today would be called lift-off, launching the whirlwind adventure of heavier-than-air flight in which he would play an important role. In 1909 – the year he joined the RNVR – Blériot flew the Channel. He was 23 when in 1912 the unsinkable *Titanic* sank, the great loss of life mitigated only by the use of Marconi's invention of wireless telegraphy.

Much later, towards the end of his aviation career, the magic of radar had decisively changed the course of world history in the Battle of Britain; pilotless jet-propelled bombs had fallen on London, closely followed by Werner von Braun's V2 rockets; and Hiroshima and Nagasaki had been evaporated into radioactive dust as the first two atomic bombs ushered in a new era of incalculably destructive warfare.

Historical and technical change, yes, but social also. When he was still a child, women started smoking in public, socialism was the political fad of the day, Oscar Wilde had 'done time' for activities which today are legal, if not totally accepted. Reggie's life spanned the stiff and starchy mores of the late

Victorian era to the age of the Beatles, of women's lib, and of a pervasive drug culture.

Change. For Reggie Marix, his early years were a time of change so rapid, so all-encompassing, and taking place on so many fronts that our own age seems almost pedestrian by comparison. And from then on the pace hardly slackened until retirement was upon him, and the world settled into the terrifying mould of the Cold War, a precarious balance which lasted more than twenty years after he died, and which immobilised east and west into a stultifying ice age.

But the most sweeping of these changes was the global reorientation of power away from the Pax Britannica which had endured throughout the nineteenth century, a fragmentation and regrouping which was well under way as Reggie grew from boyhood to manhood. James Morris again:

> In 1905 a Liberal Government came to power in London, under Henry Campbell-Bannerman. With its advent, the New Imperialism died: it was the end of Jingo – what the new Prime Minister had once called 'the vulgar and bastard imperialism of irritation and provocation and aggression . . . of grabbing everything even if we have no use for it ourselves'. The British people, Edward Grey said, were back to normal. This was fortunate, for by now Salisbury's threatening 'aggregation of human forces' seemed more menacing every year. There was war in the air, not simply the running colonial war in which the British had been engaged for a century or more, but the greater international conflict which their own dominant power had so long prevented. All the symptoms were brewing; economic rivalries, patriotic frustrations, the ambitions of leaders, dynastic squabbles, the general sense that an epoch was disintegrating and could only be cleared away by violence.

The epoch that was disintegrating was that of Reggie's youth. That it 'could only be cleared away by violence' was the driving principle behind his attack on Dusseldorf, his capture of the Baron, and – after twenty years of fragile peace – his command of 18 Group Coastal Command and Ferry Command.

Within a few years that disintegration dramatically affected great swathes of the world's populations. Growth of German military might was a major cause of the First World War, which involved almost all of Europe, much of the Middle East, parts of Africa, and revolutionary Russia. It saw the participation of General Pershing's American troops in the later battles of the Western Front. Submarine warfare outstripped the British Fleet's ability to respond effectively; the Navy's traditional role of keeping the sea lanes open was almost unattainable in the face of this ungentlemanly weapon. The sinking of the *Lusitania* played a role in embroiling the United States into a European conflict.

As Reggie's career developed into that of a fully professional, war-tested officer of the brand new Royal Air Force, Britain was experiencing the after-effects of the loss of the flower of its manhood. Burdened – impoverished, almost – by the huge debts incurred by the war, the country found its economic and military power losing ground to several countries growing at a faster pace: the United States, domestically almost unaffected by the 14-18 war; Germany, where Nazism was creating a new and dangerous threat to world peace in a resurgent nation; even far-off Japan had its eye on Asian hegemony.

World War Two saw even greater fragmentation of the old power structures. Virtually the whole world was at war. The old Empire changed completely and forever. Hong Kong, Singapore, Burma, all swept away by a distant Far Eastern Power. Canada, Australia, New Zealand protected by the overwhelming might of the United States.

After hostilities ended, the old order had changed out of all recognition. With Reggie's retirement years, India – the jewel

in the crown for centuries – became independent and parti-
tioned. The African possessions all assumed (with varying lack
of success) the burdens of autonomous nationhood. Malaysia,
Singapore, Malta – self-governing all of them, although many
countries of the old Empire elected to remain as part of a loose-
knot British Commonwealth. Even staunch Australia, whose
troops had fought with amazing skill and gallantry at Gallipoli
where Reggie had fought in the air above them, and whose
Prime Minister, Robert Menzies as late as 1953 considered himself 'British to my boot-straps', appreciated the *realpolitik* of new
defence alliances and allowed the older loyalties slowly to fade.

Reggie's story ends in 1966 in a world so utterly different
from that into which he was born that the mind has to stretch
to conceive of the contrast. Britain had been swept from the
certainties of an unchallengeable Great Britain in those final
Victorian years to the Cold War anxieties of an economically
troubled country, a strong member of NATO, but of little
other material significance on the global scene. He lived his life
against a backdrop of breathtakingly rapid change. In aviation,
during two world wars his tiny Sopwith Tabloid was replaced
by the Meteor and Canberra jets, his twenty-pound Dusseldorf
bombs by airborne nuclear weapons. In peacetime, he was a
teenager when the Wright brothers made their first stumbling
steps into the air, but towards the end of his life he could have
bought a ticket to fly across the Atlantic in Concorde at twice
the speed of sound.

Tempora mutantur, nos et mutamur in illis. Times change, and
we change with them. True of all those who need to keep up
with a changing world to remain successful in their profession.
True certainty of Reggie Marix, as his leadership remained
unchanging on the shifting sands of technical and strategic
development.

Yet at the core of the man were some unchangeable funda-
mentals.

He had a wide-ranging artistic, inventive, and creative streak. He wrote, as we have seen, with a delightful deft touch of humour and irony. He played the piano to the delight of all his friends and acquaintances. He was fluent in French, a by-product of his time at the Sorbonne. He understood music. He had mastered the art of hypnotism. It would be going too far to say that he was a Renaissance man: his commitment to his Service would not allow him the time to deserve that epithet. But he was a far cry from the unfeeling automaton who is often the popular caricature of the military man.

He was skilled in the techniques not only of flying, at which he excelled, but also in the development of ways of making his Service more effective – the novel approach to the air defence of Malta, for example. He did more than change with the times; he kept ahead of them.

He was a most gregarious and social man, with friends and acquaintances drawn from a broad worldwide spectrum. He was called upon by the highest levels (Winston Churchill, for instance, in World War One). He was able to command the respect and admiration of French-speaking academics in Canada in World War Two. He was in great demand by hosts and hostesses whenever a social gathering was being planned.

He had an iron self-discipline, which only those who knew the nature of his grievous injury could have been aware of. Pain constantly by his side, only such *maîtrise de soi* could have enabled him to stay on an even emotional keel. He had the gift of making those around him feel that they, not he, were the centre of attention. In some way known only to himself, he managed to harness his pain to the enhancement of his own personality.

He was a leader. His power of leading people did not manifest itself in just one act of bravery or devotion, but over the long haul. From his tiny force in France, in action against the Baron, to the huge spider's web of Transport Command in Montreal, his leadership shone through.

He was a man of his time, and a man ahead of his time. But above all, he was a *man* in the best chivalric sense or the term. He is remembered not just for his exploits, in the air and on the ground. Rather, he is remembered for the way his civilised values combined with his trained warrior instincts to produce a gentleman of the kind which, in our day, seems to be in short supply.

Air Vice Marshal R. L. G. Marix, CB, DSO, RAF, can most succinctly be summed up by Shakespeare's words in *Julius Caesar*:

> His life was gentle, and the elements
> So mixed in him that Nature might stand up
> And say to all the world, 'This was a man!'

Bibliography

General Works

BELL-DAVIES, VICE ADMIRAL RICHARD: *Sailor in the Air.* London: Parker Davies, 1967

CHAMIER, J A: *The Birth of the Royal Air Force.* London: Sir Isaac Pitman & Sons, 1943

CHURCHILL, WINSTON S: *The Second World War. Volume II: Their Finest Hour.* London: Cassell and Co Ltd, 1949
The Second World War. Volume IV: The Hinge of Fate. London: Cassell and Co Ltd, 1951

CREAGH & HUMPHRIES: *The VC and the DSO.* London: Standard Art Book Co.

DEIGHTON, LEN: *Bomber.* London: Triad Grafton Books, 1978

DRAPER, MAJOR CHRISTOPHER, DSC: *The Mad Major.* Air Review Ltd, 1962

EVERETT, SUSANNE et al: *Wars of the 20th Century.* London: Bison Books, 1985

GRAHAM-WHITE, CLAUDE & HARPER, HARRY: *Aircraft in the Great War.* London: T Fisher Unwin, 1915

HENDRIE, ANDREW: *Seek and Strike.* William Kimber, 1983

HEZLET, VICE ADMIRAL SIR ARTHUR, KBE, CB, DSO, DSC: *Aircraft and Sea Power.* New York: Stein and Day, 1970

179

LINECAR, HOWARD: *Aeroplanes of World War I.* London: Ernest Benn Limited, 1961

MARCUS, GEOFFREY: *Before the Lamps Went Out.* George Allen & Unwin Ltd, 1965

MORRIS, JAMES: *Farewell the Trumpets: An Imperial Retreat.* Faber and Faber, 1978

PHELAN, JOSEPH A: *Aircraft and Flyers of the First World War.* Cambridge: Patrick Stephens, 1974

POPHAM, HUGH: *Into Wind.* London: Hamish Hamilton, 1969

RALEIGH, WALTER & JONES, H A: *The War in the Air* (Volumes I-VI). Oxford: The Clarendon Press, 1922–1937

ROBERTSON, BRUCE: *Sopwith – The Man and his Aircraft.* Air Review Ltd, 1970

SAMSON, AIR COMMODORE CHARLES RUMNEY, CMG, DSO, AFC, RAF: *Fights and Flights.* London: Ernest Benn Limited, 1930

TAYLOR, A J P: *English History 1914-1945.* Oxford University Press 1965

TAYLOR, JOHN W R: *A History of Aerial Warfare.* Hamlyn, 1974

TUCHMAN, BARBARA: *The Guns of August.* New York: Macmillan Publishing Co Inc, 1962